A Master Teacher's Secrets
to
Accelerated Golf Performance

A Master Teacher's Secrets

to

Accelerated Golf Performance

Most Golfers Learn the Game Backwards

Joe Thiel
PGA Master Golf Professional

To order additional copies of this book, contact:
Xlibris Corporation
1-888-795-4274
www.Xlibris.com
Orders@Xlibris.com
58961

Contents

"Finally, learn what took us forever to learn through these amazing short-game foundational principles first. Incredible and smart!" Bill Rogers (British Open Champion)

Joe Thiel has been considered by many as one of our nation's top teachers.

He was one of the original PGA Master golf professionals and has received numerous teaching awards. His vast knowledge of accelerated performance has produced some of the finest players around the world. His instruction has touched players from all cultures and still does today as his World Wide Golf School programs continue to operate in many countries. He is the lead master instructor of the Mizuno Golf Schools and Mizuno Golf Academies worldwide that have over one hundred active teachers and coaches. His trademark performance programs have been considered by many to be the ultimate in golf accelerated performance instruction.

Now for the first time, you will be able to learn, read, and understand what he considers to be the only true incremental way to learn the game from foundations forward.

Inside you will learn:

- Why you're learning the game backwards
- An accelerated order that the game must be learned and relearned regardless of what level of golfer you are
- The body's golf-specific, setup balance system and the direct reflection it has in producing solid, full-swing fundamentals
- Tested proof from hundreds of players who immediately improved before ever being introduced to long-game mechanics when taught these foundational short game principles first
- Concepts of setting proper sternum tilts and stacked balances that will immediately impact your game

- **Unusual and tested irrefutable grip pressure points that are necessary to understand and the positive results they will bring**
- **Principles of motion that are nearly impossible to learn conventionally**
- **What he has taught about the lower body for years that you may have never heard of before that will have an immediate and positive impact on your game**
- **The "Field Harmony Flow System" that was researched and developed in Asia**
- **The system of timing sequences of the lower and upper body. No more trying to slow the hips down or speeding up the arms to get in sequence**

May these simple truths used in our everyday instruction and coaching have a direct, immediate, and positive influence in your golf journey.

FOREWORD

I am quite sure that I have never come across anyone as passionate, as enthusiastic, and as committed as Joe Thiel. My first meeting with Joe occurred in San Antonio, Texas, my home; and in an instant, it seemed as though we had known each other forever. I can confidently say that a finer friend a man could not find. I feel fortunate to be able to compose a foreword for Joe's book, and what an incredible collection of knowledge he has put together.

He has invested a lifetime in developing a sophisticated approach to learning the great game of golf, and this investment is very well documented in this instruction book. Much of his instruction discusses the importance of feel through outstanding use of pressure points, body formatting, and plane loading. As a feel player myself and I believe every great player as well, we know the benefits of tapping into the feel of the golf club in the hands. The difference here is that everyone can finally learn simply what took us forever to learn in short order through the short-game foundational principles first. Incredible and smart. I like the fact that he shares with students the most important drills and how they relate to eventually forming natural and instinctive fundamentals that cannot be refuted. All of today's great players diligently use drills in some form or another; and you will learn how these amazing foundation drills encourage you to play instinctive, intuitive, automatic golf.

Joe teaches and coaches the game with incredible passion and energy, and beyond his teaching, he loves to pass on important life lessons. Proof of his teaching expertise is the many wonderful elite juniors, all-American college players, professional champions, and quality individuals he has taught and led out into the world.

Having grown up in the great state of Texas playing golf, I, like many others, were aware of the great golf teacher Harvey Penick and the influence he had on the game of golf. Joe Thiel's approach to teaching very much lines up with Harvey's ways: *Short game first*, learning the fundamentals and applications of the short game, and then allowing them to form up the motion of the golf swing. I like how his explanation of blending these foundational truths into a "unique flow system" of how to play without foundation thought creates a harmony that every player can achieve for themselves.

Joe provides easy-to-understand information about this learning process, and if followed closely, many will learn and relearn orderly foundational blocks. He is very thorough in his descriptions of the basics, and this will provide the foundation for a good, solid golf swing and golf game.

Joe's phenomenal passion and wisdom for teaching and coaching this great game of ours encourages students to learn the basic golf swing in the correct order to become more accomplished players. His very disciplined philosophy bleeds this passion, and I know that any golfer at any level can greatly benefit from the study of these principles.

Bill Rogers
British Open Champion

Joe's forward or backward or learning the game backward. But I guess I learned it the right way because I started with Joe way back in the day! Joe Thiel has been my friend and coach for nearly ten years now. Joe has a passion for the game that cannot be matched. He brings fire and intensity to every session that I have had with him. You can't help but feed off of him. I wonder if Joe has ever woken up on the wrong side of the bed, *just one day*, like the rest of us.

For over ten years, I have gone from a decent high school player and grown into what some consider "one of the world's better players." I went from barely making my high school golf team when I was a freshman in 1997 to graduating off the nationwide tour and playing on the PGA tour in 2007.

Joe, as a master instructor, has shown me over the last ten years how to learn and understand the game from the foundation up. We have built my game in the sequence and order in which this book has been written. I guess I can say, "I have learned the game backward!" Foundations need to be built first before you can add the rest of the story. Joe knows that if you have a solid foundation you will always be able to go back and count on those foundations to correct your game. This book should be used as a road map to your golf game. If you start from the first page and apply the lessons to the end of the book, you will understand the great game of golf like you never had before.

Michael Putnam
PGA Tour member

Joe Thiel has been my coach for the last ten years. I remember my first lesson like it was yesterday; I was nine years old and had a bag full of clubs. I was ready to show off all my golfing skills and really impress my new coach. Joe set my bag off to the side, pulled out a wedge and a 9 iron, walked over to his practice green, and dumped a bucket of golf balls. He handed me the 9 iron and said show me a chip. Right then I knew this was going to be a totally new way of learning golf. By the end of the session we covered the chip, pitch, and flop shots. He sent me home with practice drills and expectations for my next lesson. My parents thought Joe's approach was a little different also; they expected him to stand at the end of a driving range and watch me hit some balls, toss out a couple of swing changes, and send me on my way. When he didn't I remember my mom questioning Joe about his approach. He explained how most golfers spend 90 percent of their time beating balls on the range and never get any better. He told her how more shots are wasted around the green and in putting. He assured her that learning all of golf's fundamentals in the short game first would help propel me to a higher level of golf than most people will ever achieve. In the past ten years under Joe's teaching methods I have won at the local, state, and national levels, with 2008 being my banner season winning four national tournaments and being named USA Rolex Junior Player of the Year. Who would have thought or dreamed a kid from Lacey, Washington, could achieve these honors? Joe did. This is just the beginning; Joe and I have bigger dreams and expectations to reach. I know if others following Joe's methods are willing to work hard they can also achieve great things.

Cameron Peck
United States Junior Amateur Champion
United States Rolex Player of the Year 2008

Joe Thiel is a man of integrity and intense professionalism. Studying Joe's book adds a whole new dimension to learning the truth of the game and applying it. Joe has distinguished himself as a teacher of the game to students of all levels. His methods are remarkably ingenious. They have been tested in the fire of competition and are proven strong and applicable to not only the serious competitive golfer, but the beginner as well. Joe communicates the game in the way it should be progressively taught. He really knows what he's talking about from years of personal instruction and study. His progressive methods of building the golf swing from the green to the tee are revolutionary and a marvelous resource for both the teacher and the student.

Wally Armstrong
PGA Tour player, teacher, and writer

In my twenty-eight years as a health-care professional dedicated to a specialty in golf, I have met and worked with hundreds of our nation's top golf instructors. However, the individual from whom I have personally learned the most and have developed the greatest respect for as a golf instructor and as a leader is Joe Thiel. Besides his extraordinary credentials as a master PGA professional and top 100 instructor with over thirty-seven years of successful teaching experience, Joe has consistently demonstrated the highest levels of personal integrity, commitment to his students, and passion for teaching that I have ever known.

Joe takes the personal responsibility to make certain that every student is properly exposed to every one of the essential ingredients for optimal success and achievement of their goals. He is closely networked with the leading professionals in their respective areas of expertise from all over the country who will be used as resources for support as necessary to attain the most efficient performance results. He is a master at identifying the learning style that is best for each golfer and adapting his approach to gain maximum communication levels that facilitate greater understanding of the methods for optimal and efficient skill development.

Most impressive to me, however, and a method that I have personally incorporated in my own work, is how Joe thoroughly interviews each and every student before a mutual decision is made to begin working with a student. Joe really wants to be in touch with the heart and soul of each student (and their family) that he chooses to instruct. He knows that success in golf and success in life depends upon the strength of relationships. When his relationship with each student is developed to the level that trust and belief are unconditionally strong, then any challenge on the golf course and in life can be overcome.

Consequently, I strongly encourage you to read this great work that is set before you that will not only astonishingly quickly impact your game, but also impact your life in a very positive way. I give Joe my highest endorsement as a professional instructor and as a human being.

Paul Callaway, PT, PhD
PGA Tour's first PT

MY GRATEFUL JOURNEY

As a youngster I was born and raised in Sharon, Pennsylvania, a city of almost twenty thousand people. It was here that my life and my destiny were touched by many positive influences, and little did I know that many of my life choices and character were formed. In our community there had lived a man and wife that through their care and generosity touched the lives of nearly every single person in one way or another. Through their love, foresight, generosity, and care, Mr. and Mrs. Frank Buhl presented to the city of Sharon acreage for huge parks and also created my gift, a nine-hole golf course. Obviously, like most children growing up in our blue collar city, I could not afford the expensive game of golf, but through Mr. Buhl's generous gift, this nine-hole course was free for all youngsters as it still is today, and I wore out my welcome. With old Sam Snead signature, borrowed golf clubs, I would be there at 5:30 AM on summer days and did not return until the church bells rang at their 5:30 PM. From the time I was ten years old I knew, not only that I would, at all costs, become a golf professional, but also that this daily practice provided a way to get out of all chores—to the consternation of my two brothers and sister. Yes, I knew that this was my calling, and having played so many make-believe matches with the great Snead and Hogan (never once losing, of course), I had "game" as they say in today's jargon. My sights were set to become the next Palmer and dethrone all current and future champions. The early influences were set in motion and with several other very important mentors in our community, including my brothers and sister who assisted and guided me. I never looked back but just followed my dreams.

The basic point of this message is my gratefulness to Mr. Buhl and his family who passed away many years before I was even born, who had the love and the foresight to make a difference to young people in our communities. Their philanthropy and Godly influence made it possible for me to capture my dreams and also taught me, more importantly, Christ-like character that has been the backbone of my life and teaching career. The Buhl family passed on to me and to countless other young and old alike in our communities, the opportunity to make a difference in life for every single person we come in contact with. I learned early through these gifts, along with the mentoring and teaching of so many others, that life is not just about us but really is about others and our influence in their lives. So for the goodness and kindness of the Buhls that cared for all people that live in and even pass through our communities, I salute the Godly influence they shared and continue to share with me. They have influenced me to strive to walk for others on this earth and become the best human being, golf instructor, learner, character developer, mentor, and friend possible. I want to personally thank God for creating such a couple willing to give, care, and mentor so many of us then and today as the gift goes on.

Joe Thiel

INTRODUCTION

It is hard to believe that I have been so fortunate to instruct the great game of golf for so many years. What a joy and a privilege it has been to be involved with so many lives through the game. For all of you that continue to desire to learn, I salute you. For this desire sets you apart and it is our job as instructors and life coaches to make sure you're on the right learning road.

This book was born out of my relentless pursuit of study. Study so I could assist thousands of golfers to learn to play the greatest game on earth in the most orderly, competent, and simplest way possible. Not just play the game, but also to learn how to accelerate each students development, building an uncluttered systematic golf foundation that will always be reliable throughout their golfing life.

The average golfer around the world has a 20+ handicap, and the USGA (United States Golf Association) states that there is less than a two-shot progress in the improvement level for the last many years. The question that we all have to ask ourselves is why is this so? If you pooled each of the nearly forty thousand teachers in our world today, I doubt you would even find one that would say that their students do not improve. If that is the case, then why don't golfers play at a higher level? I think there are several possible reasons, ranging from finding the necessary practice time it takes or committing to a well-matched instructor, to a lack of commitment in order to improve. However I have found more than all the above combined and right from the beginning: *Golfers have spent the majority of their time learning the game backwards.* The typical way of learning has been to start students right from the beginning with a midlofted golf club in their instruction class or private session. The typical goal is an attempt to learn how to move their body and golf club throughout the full-swing motion. Even the player who has played for several years and continues to take instruction does the same thing. He or she goes to the practice facility or golf course and attempts to learn once again the full-swing motion, continuously adjusting and readjusting one thing after another. This type of practice development really never changes much of anything and tends to cement poor habits that are sure to show up in any type of pressure situation. Year after year the same scenario plays itself out again with the USGA, stating that we are not really improving that much. Golfers have hit that strong wall, and most players never break through. My passion and challenge over these many years is to relentlessly pursue simple acceleration education principles in all areas of this game, creating a bona fide fool-proof, hyper-accelerated, and well-mapped system of learning for every single student that walks through the instruction door.

With that said, well over two decades ago I started experimenting with students by starting golf development programs with several "foundational building blocks of instruction" beginning with the short game first. In those beginning years, I took the time to document and compare similar handicap levels with those that I started with in the long game as well, compared their growth of development and the results from those first few years was remarkable. *All levels ranging from beginners to low-handicap golfers displayed much faster improvements in all aspects of the full swing ball striking when first taught foundation principles first in the short game.*

I knew then that I would institute these steps in my teaching for all players. Since those early days I have refined it much more and the student learning acceleration has been dramatic. These simple laws and concepts of motion cannot be refuted and taught this simple way are easily attainable.

My hope is that I can say it well enough on paper that it will translate as easy for you readers as it does in person. My tendency as an instructor is to often repeat the points that I wish for each student to maximize and this is smart in person but terrible in a book form. My hope is that you can read between poor jargon and repeated phrases and imagine learning as if we were one-on-one in the first of several 1.5-hour sessions. To also make the read a bit easier, I have written this work for the right-handed player. You growing number of lefties out there can adjust to this unfortunate and unfair slight.

In order for students to learn these irrefutable concepts it is important that they be revisited time and time again. Since I am not there hounding each of you, it is your job and that of a helper, whether it be a teacher or another set of eyes, to do the same thing. Stay on it and make it part of your everyday practice session. These frequent revisits will *develop the necessary mental connections and subconscious habit that make good technique and foundation instinctive.* You will find the learning and development so much fun and play remarkably better. It has been proven time and time again, "So tape up your ankles and strap on your boots," as my friend Bill Rogers says, " and let's get this show down the road."

THE SHORT-SHOT TEST

The short game is a pretty darn accurate indicator of what is happening in the full swing. This is one of the principle methods many tour players and outstanding amateurs use to locate their swing deficiencies and return their out-of-sync game back to fluid again. Using the short game to find swing anomalies works perfectly as it allows each player to instinctively feel micro timings, clubface angles, pressure points, path, rhythm, and tempo much easier than they could by using a full swing. It is generally simpler to narrow in on specifics in a shorter motion then a larger one.

Using this same tour-tested principle that many great players of this game employ, many years ago, I wondered how this concept would work with *all* levels of players that we teach. So we did early experiments with hundreds of amateur players, videotaping their full swing with some pretty rudimentary equipment and without any instruction. Next I proceeded to teach four private, short-game sessions only, focusing on the simple short-game foundational principles that are in this book. Several weeks later we re-taped each student's full swing without long-game instruction of any kind. Once again we found that the long-game swing improvements for each of those students was *phenomenal*. Some of the dynamic natural laws of motion and leverage that are simple habit to a lucky few, made their way right into the automatic, full-action movement of these students. This allowed the body to develop its swing more naturally and athletically because it was first broken down into smaller parts for an efficient and tangible dissection. If what I saw back then was not true 100 percent of the time, then this book and certainly the foundation of my instruction would not have been implemented.

I would like to share these same principles to assist you in developing the techniques of your long game with these "more natural" short-game absolutes. This proven information will surely create a more efficient and finally straightforward, uncomplicated way of accelerating your learning; taking you much closer to your playing, scoring, and "fun potential."

While it is true that to the eye there are many players with different-looking golf swings who make a living playing this sport, close scrutiny shows that each of these players has important common denominators that *cannot be refuted*. The surprise to most is that all these common denominators are instinctively available to each of you.

Let's first start with

PREPOSTURE, SETUP, AND GRIP

The short game's posture and setup correlates specifically to that of the long game. If you are able to learn this component alone, your long game will be positively enhanced. There are four main angles of setup that you need to learn well before you go any further in your practice. I feel confident saying that *most have not learned these profound angles in their entirety* and without them your golf swing will be a mixture of compensatory movements. Now don't get frustrated here because you have most likely read countless articles about the setup. There is pertinent information that is foundational and can't be missed that will have a profound impact on your game.

Grip Discussion

It is absolutely impossible to discuss any area of swing, short game, or putting without first locating and balancing out our hold on the golf club as it pertains to *impact*. Everything we do in producing ball flight is directly related to our body, arm, and hand configurations at impact; and if you can learn how to properly configure your grip and setup, you will remove many possible negative variables. This "foundation principle" is basic to every shot, chip, and putt we hit.

In our first short-game chip session I ask all students to show me their current setup focusing on their grip. I then ask them to demonstrate how they perceive that to look at impact. Nearly every time each player then regrips and adjusts forearms to demonstrate their impact position. That is because a flat left-wrist position at impact requires a different grip, forearm and face positioning than the grip they originally had. Notice in the pictures below the changes in the forearms and also the right-hand grip position adjustment of the student in the photos.

[Address to impact with a negative small adjustment
to accommodate impact.]

[A good grip can easily translate into a sound impact position
without adjustments.]

A sound grip is a whole lot easier to deliver instinctively square at impact and requires zero compensation. This is a huge foundational building block that proceeds right into the long game. The unusual grips that many people use restrict the natural setting of the golf club and hinder all possible consistency, making it imperative that we address it. It seems that most players are very uncomfortable changing or adjusting their current grip in the full swing. Therefore I prefer to demonstrate, through short-game chips, that modifications to grip can be much more easily attained than you would think. Not only is it easier to make changes in grip for the long game by breaking it down into smaller shots, it's also more beneficial for your short game as well, and you will see how.

In our first session with students we spend an hour and a half on little shots and modify the grip to create different types of spins and trajectories. This enables the player to understand how different grips can be used for all kinds of shots in the short game and are relatively easy to be comfortable with. Realizing that many greats of the game have more than one type of hold on the golf club with these short shots helps students realize the benefit of little adjustments in grip. I will even have students hit a few chips with their putting grip to catch a feel of how this type of hold makes it really easy to be consistent as well. So with a sound grip we see how the clubface, required angle pressures, and hold on the golf club must be linked together so that instinctive movements are enhanced generating consistency.

Your unique hold

You can find your unique body structure and grip by standing straight up with your head, neck, shoulders, upper and lower back, and legs all in a comfortable straight line. Start by standing against a wall with as much of the upper body touching as possible. Feel as if there are little or no gaps from your upper shoulders all the way down to your lower back and rear. With your arms hanging straight down from your shoulder sockets, you will find a pretty good starting point of your natural left- and right-hand hang. Using the wall helps student's avoid rounding or slouching their shoulders forward which would create a different (false) look of the hand and arm hang. At this point I place a club in the fingers of my student's left hand first with the pad of the left hand on top of the club. The hand will face the same direction as it would without the club, in a comfortable and natural hang position. I also put a second club in the fingers of their right hand and have students bring these two golf clubs forward to look at them.

A common response is that they feel normal when the club is held to the side, but when it is moved forward toward a swing setup it feels somewhat unusual. Once students become comfortable with the feeling and have a solid and natural grip on the club, they proceed to add the right hand to the left via an overlapping or interlocking connection.

There are several slightly different-looking grips that work without compensations and may differ for each individual. What feels correct and solid for one player may not be the case for another. Teachers have their own preferences for grips; one that will contribute to a powerful golf swing without needed compensatory movements. I am no exception. I think all teachers have experimented with many types of holds but most come back to the finger-type grip. I believe that the club does belong in the fingers of the left hand and runs diagonally from the second knuckle of the forefinger to the base knuckle of the pinky with the heel pad on top as shown below. Also since we are looking for strong forward swing delivery angles which produce powerful ball and clubhead speed, these tasks are very difficult to accomplish without a finger type of hold.

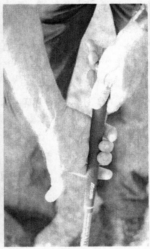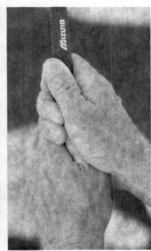

This is the hold/grip that facilitates on plane impact position as well with proper use of the left- and right-hand wrists. For the average right-handed player, this means that the left hand would show 2+ knuckles as you look down at the grip with the right hand inner palm facing the target. The right-hand grip is also held in the fingers and not the palm. This type of hold will help assist the natural wrist hinging that is necessary in all shots and also promotes the hand and arm gravity hang positions described earlier.

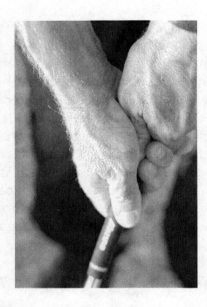

Many players who have unnatural grips struggle to have that same grip at impact. I often find that when I ask them to show me the impact position, they adjust, slide, or regrip their fingers to accomplish it. However there are some good players that have employed unusual cocking motions and wrist sets in the backswing in order to accommodate their unusual hold on the golf club. What is most important is that your grip on that golf club should allow you to deliver a powerful, on-plane, square clubface at impact without a hint of reorganization. If any compensation should occur in order to square the clubface, then inconsistencies will follow.

POSTURE, SETUP, AND ALIGNMENT FOUNDATIONS

To demonstrate the first principles of the short-game chipping setup, let's start with your feet about the width of your clubhead just a few inches apart. Use your golf club to measure this as illustrated.

From a perfectly square stance turn *only* the toes of your feet to the left just a few degrees and locate 60-65 percent of your weight on your target side foot. I think it is also important to learn to chip from a square setup at first. Many players throughout the history of golf have chipped from square setups as well, and this will also help prevent a need to swing in-to-out dramatically on chips. The club will work along your body lines on a normal swing plane, whereas the slightly open stance automatically creates an out-to-in, across-the-body motion.

Next bend your knees just slightly and finally bend forward from the hip sockets.

This bend at the hip sockets is vitally important but is almost always a misunderstood *foundational block* in the full golf swing and also in the short game. So let's take some time here to discuss and learn it correctly right from the start. Since your body's forward bend of the hips and upper trunk toward the golf ball dramatically affects ball flight, path, grip, and even health, it is important to understand it. Set your club aside and place a couple of your fingers in front of your hip sockets as illustrated below. As you bend forward, maintain your upper and lower spine angle without bending or curving the midback area.

With your fingers you will feel the hips set as you bend forward about 20-25 degrees from vertical maintaining your 60—40 weight balance on the target side foot.

[This drill will help you finally feel a proper hip set.]

If you have not rounded the upper regions of your back, you will likely have experienced a new sensation. Many say right in that first short-game session that it feels as if they are for the first time grounded or solid in their setup. It also will feel like your rear has projected out a little more than before. The grip you discovered when standing straight up hangs in the same pattern when you bend forward. This "pelvic tilt" as I have termed it, is essential to great ball striking. Several years ago I devoted the time to create a DVD and video on this subject alone. This hip flex and hold is probably the most "missed" and misunderstood teaching fundamental. I would say that most folks bend forward from the stomach and midspine area, resulting in the rounding of the mid and upper back; scooting their stomach forward, widening their shoulder blades as they reach down toward the golf ball.

[Poor, slouchy posture full swing position.] [Much better hip flex and back angles.]

Your job as you bend forward from these hip sockets is to maintain a normal "tension-free flat back," shoulder blades drawn together in a neutral position with a soft and comfortable arm extension to the ball.

Let's move on and we will discuss this in more detail later. With this new hip/back grounded sensation, take the time to flatten your lower back by rotating your pelvis a bit forward, removing lower-back cupping. Cupping the lower back will also cause the need for much compensation during the golf swing and also trend toward injuries. I have had many young students who have cupped their backs, and with a little practice, they learned how to roll tilt their pelvises forward to produce a perfect tilt. Ball flight, speed, and consistency improved with every practice session.

[From cupped back to a solid flat back position makes a world of difference.]

Finally I prescribe a slight pre-impact setup with the knees, hips, and legs. This has proven to be important to thousands of students, so don't miss it. This pre-impact set finds your target side knee a fraction taller and the target side hip turned slightly open.

[Ever so slight pre-impact lower body demonstrated here at setup.]

This preset has been invaluable in my instruction, as it demonstrates to all students how the knees and hips move even in little simple chips. One of the daily homework assignments is to have students *shadow swing* in front of a mirror at home to watch and train motions of the body. Focus on how the left knee gets a bit taller and the hips gradually and naturally turn a bit open as they move through the chip. Repeat the movement and begin to transfer that feeling into the subconscious mind, and it will soon become a natural habit. Once it does become habit we can then rely on it in pressure circumstances to instinctively deliver.

THE POSTURE HOP

There is a great and simple way of checking on your posture with what we call the posture hop. Once you feel you're in a solid-set position, hop a tiny bit off the ground without adjusting your body's angle and knee bends when you land. See if you find yourself in exactly the same position that you started or if your body reorganizes its natural balance to a slightly different position.

The natural landing location is the perfect balance for you, and with practice, will deliver the golf club in your most powerful and on-plane position. When many of the players that I coach are out of sync, sometimes just this little posture check can be all that they need to get in balance and rhythm. As a side note we suggest most students enroll in a well-balanced martial arts program. The prime foundation of these disciplines is balance and stability at all times statically and in motion. The arts are a parallel companion to golf, as they will help you learn how to deliver power in balance. The arts have also proven to develop confidence, discipline, and competitive toughness. If you are a competitive player then take a serious look into martial arts programs.

[Student Cameron Peck in action and receiving his black belt.]

SHOULDER BLADES AND ROTATOR MUSCLES

The rotators, better known as the rotator cuffs, are the four muscles that stabilize arms and shoulders from setup to finish. Unfortunately you may be one of the many guilty "shoulder reachers." This means that you bend forward correctly but then overextend the arms and shoulders by releasing upper back and midscapular/shoulder blade muscles to reach the ball. This overreach will produce a negative rounding of the upper back ultimately destroying the full swing. This rounded look also produces a different hand/grip configuration at address, and therefore makes consistent and instinctive impact impossible.

[Many have established this poor shoulder reach making the game so complicated.]

Another misunderstood term in the long game is *extension*. This golf term has thrown many students off and is responsible in my opinion for much confusion. Proper extension is the length of your arms and shoulders at address maintained in that length tension free during the backswing. Many golfers misunderstand this term and try to extend their arms and shoulders on the backswing. To do so they overextend the midscapular and upper back muscles, causing many severe errors.

[An improper shoulder reach.]

An improper extension of the shoulder blades and midscapular muscles coupled with weak abdominals and spine rotator muscles result in many poor shots. The upper back and spine angles break down and lose their ability to hold during the swing. Students that have this difficulty need to learn how to stay neutral, or "soft straight" as we call it, and not protracted away from the ribs. A simple drill to grasp this feeling in the back area is from a standing position, softly interlock your fingers with palms touching behind your back and relax your shoulders. From here bend forward with as little tension as possible into your address position noticing the lack rounding in your upper back region.

[Back sequence daily practice routine]

If you have discomfort with the upper back rounding, practice without a club with the palms behind you feeling the movement back and forth. After several repetitions, try creating the same feeling with a wedge in hand moving back and forth with half-size swings. The shoulder blades hold with as little tension as possible during the motion. Many students in the beginning few short-game sessions say for the first time they can feel how the back is actually used in the swing, and it feels surprisingly good right from the start.

[Nice-looking tension free natural extension is what you are after.]

Sharing this important information in the long game first makes it very frustrating for students and it is rare to see anyone who is an over-reacher improve quickly. Instead, if you begin to practice correct posture in the short game, it can be easily incorporated into the full swing. Learning these changes in simple chips and pitches develops instinctive habits for you and have immediate and positive ramifications in your long game. It doesn't take much to grasp this, just the discipline to learn it first in the short game.

Years of experience in this area have taught me, however, that those of you who have had that sizable rounded upper back need to make your adjustments small and step-by-step. I depend on simple morning stretches and an exercise program to help students quickly eliminate this poor posture. Included in the end of this book are *morning and pregolf warm-up principles* that are designed to influence this technique. If you have this problem, be sure to take a good look at this area of the book. In our schools we take this concept even further for the "motivated" player and teach what our mothers always used to tell us about our posture. You should carry this practice into your daily life; and practice your posture in sitting, standing, and walking positions. This daily practice not only leads to better posture when playing the game, but also changes people dramatically including overall long-term physical and mental health.

BALANCE

It is important that each student also understands what "stacked balance" is and the positive effects that this balance will have on your golf game. This balance simply means that shoulders and knees are somewhat stacked up over the front/balls of the feet or in an athletically balanced vertical line.

[Stacked balance with shoulders, knees and feet all in athletic posture.]

This "centering," as we also term it, plays a major role in great ball striking and needs to be located by all students. There are two balance points in the body, one being near the naval area, and the other near the top of the sternum. When these two balance points are set correctly, the body is in a rock solid position of balance. Many tend to bend so far forward in the upper regions of the body that the shoulders are well in front of the feet. This will cause many full-swing imbalances and students will then have to make swing compensations to even make good contact.

[Overleaning the upper torso.] [Stacked correctly over the feet.]

This overlean of the upper torso additionally moves the address hands to an unnatural location, far too inside and under the front hang of the shoulders. This poor position makes it very tough to get to impact instinctively.

To find your athletic balance and a positive powerful setup position, practice a small posture hop, which will guarantee to stack your body well. Then try rocking this "intact setup" back and forth from heel weight to toe weight until you feel the rock solid balance on the balls of your feet (see pictures on the next page). It may be here that you finally locate your two centers of balance that we discussed earlier.

I have found through student feedback that this rocking drill does a whole lot more than just instruct balance, and as we progress in this book you also will find this to be true.

[The body balance rocking drill.]

If you continue to do this rocking drill for a bit longer you will feel it in your abs and lower back. Acquiring this new, centered balance is critical, so don't write it off. Learn it. Once you find your center balance points, you will see that someone's gentle push in different directions does not move you out of balance.

[Sound rock solid setup. Slight pre impact set, feet square, but toes slightly turned left a bit, shoulders fairly level, nice straight line from bicep to clubhead creating the pre-impact feeling.]

What we are looking for is a natural athletic balanced position that promotes all the ingredients of a powerful long game via the short game. If we can get that naturalness to come out and make it a *habit*, we are well on our way. There is *not one* person who can't have this above setup and be able to in short order deliver it to impact. For some it may take a bit longer than others, but once they have it, their game turns around in a hurry.

ARM HANG AND ADDRESS
SHAFT PLANE

For a moment here we will venture off into the arm hang of these short chips, but for the short game only as it gradually changes as the club length and swing size increase in the longer shots. In these short shots, if you would just take this new solid posture and allow your arms to just gravity drop from your shoulders, you may likely find them located a bit different then your normal address.

[Note shaft angle is just a bit lower than the forearm angles allowing for wrist hinging.]

However this is *the* premium location at least to start learning your chip technique. From this neutral hang, it is easier to choke down some on the golf club and get that feeling that the entire body is in concert with the short shot we are about to play. Sort of like the baseball batter chocking up a little on the bat for tighter control and easier contact.

The shaft angle at address also is very important as it is most productive when somewhat similar to the hanging angle of your forearms requiring less skill to make contact.

In all swings, even the short-game chips and pitches, centrifugal/ centripetal forces are present, and the shaft will tend to get a bit taller on the downswing. If yours is quite low and too deep an angle to start with, you will tend to duff these shots considerably. If you tend to hit them thin, well you've done a good job of pulling some portion of your body up to compensate duffing to produce those thin shots. Many a broken-down left arm extension at impact on full swings can be traced right back to this early development. Another good reason why spending a good deal of time right here in the short game first has its lifetime rewards for the entire game.

[As part of your pre-shot routine try this little simple step
in drill with the right hand only.]

As you complete your setup, maintain that shaft angle that you stepped in with, and you will find this angle not exactly as your forearms, but fairly close to it. Since you hold the club in your fingers it can't be the same exact angle, but again we see too many people with the shaft angle so low that the grip nearly touches their thighs, and that causes many needs for compensations.

Ball Position

Initially I teach three basic ball positions as well as three clubface positions for the short game, and they are not unlike several other teachers. Students call them their own however as numbers one to three. Typically number one and the "bread and butter position" most use when there is enough green to work with is located near the right instep. This back position along with the mentioned forward shaft lean at address will make it easy to make ball-first contact with somewhat of a steeper swing. If you have a proper amount of bounce in your wedges, the club will still skid well on the ground. Some will even move their position number one even further back outside the right foot itself. Perfectly fine, adjust these according to your comfort level. With the ball that far back, we have already adjusted the address loft of the clubhead to a much lower lofted golf club in reality or effective loft as we call it at impact.

[Ball position one off-right instep and each new ball position half a ball forward.]

Next is ball position number two and that is half a ball or more forward toward the target foot. With the same forward shaft lean of the position number one, the address loft of the wedge has effectively been changed. Finally, move to ball position number three which is another half a ball or more forward. These three positions are the starting instructional positions in early development. As each student progresses in the short-game finesse skills, they continue to develop their own ball and clubface positions to create different type shots with different spins. Most players then add many more positions, including adjustments of shaft leans, to create certain desired effects.

THE BIG-TIME, MISUNDERSTOOD STERNUM

Instructing students to use the sternum as a means of describing unique spine/shoulder tilts and bends at address is critical in the short game. Typically, most players misunderstand what 60/40 weight lean toward the target really means in these short shots. When you read that competitive players put a little more weight on the target side foot for these type shots and even in the bunkers, you also try to do the same thing. However most players mistakenly reverse the upper body at setup, resulting in 60 percent right foot and 40 percent left foot weight distribution (for right-handed players). Since the golf club is certainly more related and connected to the upper body, by doing so, you actually made your setup even worse than it was before. In fact, the bottom of the impact arc has changed on the chip/ pitch circle to a location further behind the ball causing duffed or rearranged bladed shots. Look to the picture on the next page, and you will see how many players place themselves in this mistaken posture.

For many years I tried to simplify the upper body's set position as neutral (+1 and +2) positions.

[Neutral standing position—Neutral address sternum position.]

In neutral 1 position, the sternum is slightly in front of the ball at address resulting from the ball position well back in the setup and the lower body's weight more toward the target side foot. This setup is unusual for typical players as they tend to mistakenly drop their right shoulder low and left shoulder very high. This shoulder tilt causes side bending and leaning the upper body back behind the ball. If you think this through for a minute you'll note that when we started learning the new setup, we began by standing straight up and then placing more weight on the left or target side foot then the right. From that position as you recall, we then bend over from the pelvis "straight down and straight forward." Now we did this without a club in hand at first, so the shoulders would bend forward accordingly and have no negative tilt to them. However once people put a club in their hands they tend to drop the right shoulder considerably more than the left. The right hand being the low hand on the golf club will automatically drop the shoulder to some degree.

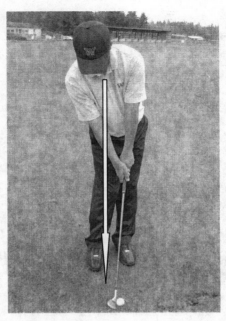

[Poor upper body setup causes many negative results.]

As you see in the poor setup above, students tend to overtilt to the right, drawing the right hand down and under which negates the positive lower body's 60/40 set up. Big problems occur from here.

Try this drill to catch this unusual but correct feeling. Practice sternum position number one, placing your hands on your grip exactly on top of and equal to each other at address. At times we even demonstrate a left hand low grip to assist students in feeling proper sternum/shoulder and spine tilt.

[Start your drill here and then with normal grip hold the shoulders
in the same position.]

Next learn to put your hands on the club without dropping your right
shoulder at all. You will notice such a change, and after hitting a few
shots you'll feel as if you can pinch these shots off concrete without
hitting fat and skulled shots.

Sternum number two is just a little more spine tilt left toward the target
which makes it feel as if your right shoulder is higher than the left. This
will most likely have an opposite feeling then the normal setup.

[Sternum # 2 position with lean in front of the ball.]

These leans serve their purposes well, making tight, muddy, hard pan, deep rough, and many more ugly lies a ton easier. Simply readjusting your address position will reduce many anxieties that you may have had for years on short pitches and chips.

As you become better at this, we then introduce at least one sternum lean in the minus positions as well. You can imagine that with more grass under the ball, it can be quite effective to have a reverse lean that has the upper body leaning ever so slightly to your right or away from the target. This opposite tilt will create a great deal more loft at impact, achieving a very high shot. During the motion it is important however to maintain these different leans and not at transition or in the forward swing adjust your upper body's lean in any way. Each student's job as I see it is to learn at least two simple sternum leans. The neutral number one and the bit stronger lean for ugly lies, number two.

Now the angle of the pelvis needs to duplicate the position of the sternum. This new positioning needs to create a much more level hip position at address and held all the way through the shot.

It is important that your sternum/pelvis positioning remains consistent and on top of or in front of the golf ball at all times in the short, basic chips. At first, practice this with the chip shot only, matching both the pelvis and sternum angles until it feels natural.

HOW IMPORTANT
IS "GRIP PRESSURE?"

Though *often* neglected, grip pressure is a *huge* important link between the body that generates power, and the golf club affected by that same power. It is imperative that hand and arm pressure does not increase or decrease much during the motion of the swing. I say much because at transition in a sound swing there may be a tiny increase of grip pressure due to the fact that the forward swing is near three times faster in time then the backswing. But the feeling we share with students is one that does not change much really at all. The hands that should act as a positive link often will negatively affect swing tempo by maintaining an average pressure on the backswing and increasing dramatically into the downswing, thus decreasing swing speed. As grip pressure increases, the body and brain naturally begin to rely on the hands to generate power. This results in the body's inability to maintain athletic natural power angles, timing and the automatically squared clubface delivered to impact.

Try this mini test. Hold a normally gripped, square-faced iron horizontally in front of you and then snap-grab that club tight. Pay close attention to the club face. It's a good test that shows the negative effects of a jerky grabbing type of swing.

As part of your daily practice, determine what your strongest and weakest amount of grip pressure is. Rating this on a scale of one to ten, find a four and practice maintaining that amount of pressure throughout the duration of the swing. Remember to pay special attention to grip pressure at the transition points of the backswing and downswing. In many sessions I will ask students to hit several chips with a three-grip pressure throughout, then a few at four, five, and so on. Each quickly discover what their number is and learn to make it their own. This drill and many other tension-monitoring drills will change your contact dramatically. Not only will grip pressure bring positive results, but also maintaining it will directly correlate to body tension. It's like a chain reaction. If your hold on the golf club is in a comfortable range then your arms, neck, and shoulders will follow suit, creating a more tension-free flow. Later we will discuss a pre-shot sequencing routine that accompanies this tension-free understanding that will transfer immediately into your mental game performance.

Take the time to learn grip pressure in those little shots first. Don't jump ahead into full shots just yet.

PRESSURE POINTS

Since pressure points in the golf swing are *paramount* to great ball striking and in my opinion cannot be refuted, each player that does not automatically have these must learn several things about them. First they must know what they are and where they are located, and second how to monitor these points starting with the *short game first* until they become *habit*. This is the easiest and most efficient way to accomplish this huge link to great golf. If each of you reading this material could climb into the body of a tremendous ball striker and feel their hands, wrists, and arms throughout the golf swing, you would all be shocked. Most of you would find the feeling completely strange since the correct feeling is not commonly discussed. The concept is the key, and once it is incorporated, you will love the results. Through years of teaching and experimentation with every imaginable thought of pressure points, I have come back time and again to these specially developed few:

For The Right-handed Player

First and foremost is the right hand's underside forefinger. In its neutral-held position, one should attempt to feel the pressure and weight of the golf club in the crease of that underside second knuckle of the forefinger; I call this the "trigger pad." Student's should feel the club load into that trigger pad on the backswing and in the forward transition, slightly "tug" that trigger pad all the way to impact. We use that feel in the full swing as well, as it gives all students (especially those that learn the game primarily kinesthetically), an immediate perfect understanding of loading and unloading on the correct plane. This sensation is a must, and it secures "lag and plane" for the rest of every players' life. **This must be established as a fundamental routine right from the start of every player's developing program. We train our students to monitor these lag pressure point components rather than making an attempt to just "hit the ball." ** This is very important but almost always a majorly missed concept by many players. There is a bit of that sensation also in the second knuckle of the middle finger of the right hand as well, and some students say they feel it in this location as much as the forefinger point. Now for those of you who have very small hands, you may note the location is just a tiny bit different than those with big hands; that is perfectly OK and you can adjust accordingly.

The second pressure point is the heel or the lifeline area of the right hand. Assuming your grip is similar to the grip we recently discussed, you will note the left-hand thumb married and snuggled into the right-hand lifeline. During the backswing initially feel that left hand thumb "loading the club on its correct plane." That correct plane is one that finds the shaft pointed right back at the golf ball, very near and parallel to the same angle as the original shaft angle at setup.

[Shaft and left-hand thumb on plane and pointed right back
at the golf ball's target line.]

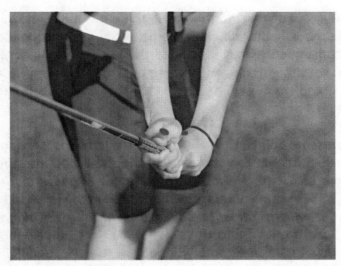

[Note the dots I placed on the two thumbs. You can use these two thumbs to feel the correct plane which is the shaft and handle pointed towards the target line continuously on the way up in the backswing.]

In transition and continuing into the forward swing, you should feel a slight soft push of that right-hand heel against the left-hand thumb and toward the left wrist. This promotes the left and right wrist to cock a bit more on the downswing as the *arms* deliver the golf club. This is a great first-time sensation for many students, as it also promotes you to deliver the club with the arms on the downswing instead of the hands snapping delivery or the body only delivery.

Many students have a tendency to now jump right into some full swing shots to capture this feel, but it must be practiced in these short shots first to develop it. My years of experience tell me that if you do this right and learn these microfeelings by making them natural here first, it will then transfer right into your long game. This is a big and contributing reason for these half-dozen short game sessions because I personally want to see some sound instinctive habits formed *first*.

I have felt that the teaching of pulling down with the last three fingers of the left hand that has been somewhat prominent the last two decades may have thrown people off. The arms surely need to be generating the forward motion not the hands. This attempt at pulling those three fingers may have actually caused many players to push the handle toward the ground with the thumbs in the early stages of the forward swing. This poor habit will cause some serious consequences. Some of these consequences have included the left-arm radius breakdown, a premature straightening of the right arm, a jerk of the timing sequences, and the dreaded cast or club throwaway as it generally is referred to.

Another pressure point is the *forefinger of the left hand,* second-knuckle area as well. Students can start to feel the shaft load into the correct swing plane using the feel of both forefinger trigger knuckles in the backswing. These same points are emphasized in the forward transition area as you *pull the pressure points toward you* (not down), while the arms take the lead into the downswing. Like all pressure points, students tend to misinterpret what these fingers should be doing, preventing many potentially great players from being very good.

Suffice it to say that a constant equal grip pressure in both hands and a monitored sensory feeling of special pressure points along with decent tempo will go a *long* way toward helping your entire game. When we instruct the short game lag and pressure point areas first, *everyone's* game changes immediately as they finally understand how power is loaded and delivered by the arms with pressure points intact and instinctively released.

I have seen students' entire game change in this area once they understood pressure points. I have taken so much time to video student after student before and right after teaching pressure points and put the two swings side-by-side. The difference is immediate. For the first time, decent plane and angles were achieved just with this little kinesthetic feeling and knowledge. Ball flight, path, and distance also changed dramatically in launch monitor testing for everyone as they embraced the correct load and reloading feelings.

A side note about these several pressure points so far is that back in the 1980s, our men's club at the golf facility I was employed with had a night each summer they called the Club Throw. It was fun to watch these crazy guys get out there after their round of golf and throw old clubs at a target. Even with old video equipment one could see how much better their instinctive motion was tossing these clubs then their normal motion hitting a golf ball. As we took this club throwing a bit further through experimentation, we found that the mind was actively seeking a means to toss these clubs at the target, generating great body movements and natural lag pressure. This feeling immediately translates into amazingly sound golf swings that are more simple and instinctive. The body's brain naturally knew that the arms were supposed to lead in the forward swing and that the old cast-type push of incorrect hands would not work if they wanted to toss that club down the fairway. It worked time and time again and was an eye-opening experience for many students when they saw this action on tape. The body simply reconfigured itself toward instinctive behaviors, and off the club went right toward the target.

Since it is paramount for each player to experience how the arms initiate the forward swing, we also spend time introducing the different possible feel sensations of the arm's initial delivery as needed. Since many have initiated the downswing sequence first with a quick move of the hips or legs, they tend then to cast these short shots and lose the timing of the sequences of the legs and arms to impact. If this is the case then we must share some of the arm delivery pressure point possibilities.

Feeling the back underside of the left forearm and/or the back of the triceps area gently pulling on plane initially in the forward swing are a couple of arm pressure point possibilities. Allowing one of these to start the transition swing without grab of the hands is an important feeling for some. To many it feels as if the shoulders held a bit as the arms initiated and that is a great and important feeling.

The final in the pressure points discussion is the amount of squeeze one employs in the right and left hand thumbs. Thumbs on the shaft are support vehicles in which to load the backswing and additionally will hopefully and naturally *carry* that larger load to impact as the arms deliver the downswing. Unfortunately most use the *thumb pads* to push the hands and clubhead toward the ground, which again destroys path and power. The correct feeling at transition should be a soft, nonpressured contact with the grip in *the underside knuckle area of the thumbs, not the pad areas*. This contact relationship with these knuckles and maintaining them during the forward swing goes a long way toward angle retention. Many years ago the thumb area became a *huge* discovery for me. Players who struggle with angles, tension, and consistent contact all "fell in love" with this on the first day of instruction in the short game. Every single player has some immediate improvement once we assist them with removing additional pressure in these thumb pads along with the feel and visuals associated with using the thumbs for plane instruction. The feel is simple, monitor a feeling of a soft four-grip pressure during the entire chip stroke, feel the underside of the thumb knuckles put pressure against the handle *toward you* on the downswing, and see the results. They are pretty darn staggering.

Pressure Point Drills and Practice

For your first drill, try placing a bit of grass just inside that second knuckle of your right-hand forefinger, enough to feel the club as it loads a bit in these short shots into that knuckle.

 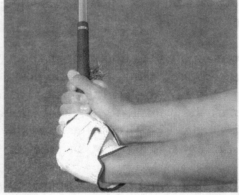

[I love this drill as it gives players for the first time a *quantified* way to not only feel the club reload on the downswing for power, but also feel it load on the right path and plane.]

Now note how the pressure on that knuckle and the grass under it feels if the club is loaded on a plane that points the handle correctly at your golf-ball target line. Note the different feeling and the pressure with the grass knuckle combination if it is loaded flat around you or too far outside away from you. Make note of which feel is correct and which is not. Try adding a bit of grass also in the left-hand forefinger second-knuckle areas and you can monitor both at the same time. I have found some students like this while others like the feeling of just one.

During the backswing use the grass as a tool to load the club against on the correct swing plane.

Even in the short chips and pitches you can feel the angle increase if you can slightly tug that grass/knuckle up toward you in transition

Also try adding a bit of grass or divot to the top of your left-hand thumb and under the heel of your right hand as shown in the pictures below.

 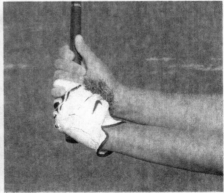

(During the backswing feel that grass and thumb combination load on the correct swing plane)

(On the forward swing feel the heel portion of your right hand softly push against the top knuckle of your left hand and a bit toward you creating a deeper angle of delivery.)

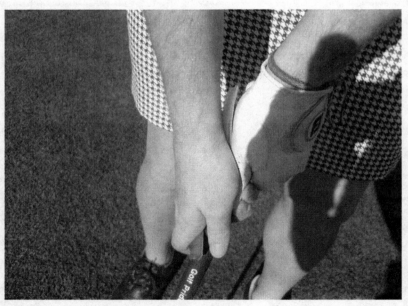

[A spongy substance we use for pressure points can also assist these feelings.]

During your chipping practice, attempt to feel those pressure points moving more *on the plane line* on the backswing. The correct plane will point the butt end of the golf club right at the ball target line. On the forward swing, monitor a consistent feel of the grass pulled from the right forefinger against the shaft up toward you and the grass pushed from the right-hand pad against that left-hand thumb toward the left wrist. Eventually do it all with a light, soft-grip pressure adding this to your everyday practice. Separate your practice using one pressure point only. After several minutes, try switching around with different pressure points until you locate the right combination for you. The idea of course is for you to start to naturally uncover the feelings that have always been there but have not been put to use. These pressure points are irrefutable, and it is our job to help you find them. These concepts are much tougher to describe in a book than in person, but a sure bet you will be able to soon feel it with smart practice and just a bit of persistence.

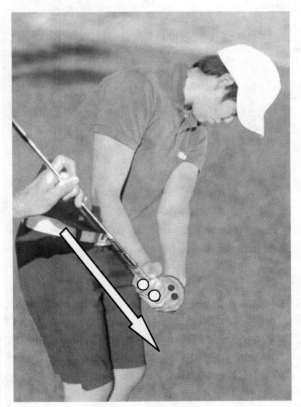

[Matching right- and left-hand forefinger knuckles and the
left-hand thumb all on the correct swing plane.]

This is a great visual and a great feel that can so easily be monitored for plane instruction for your entire game. This feel and instruction should take you all the way into all your full shots. It is so much easier than just using shafts, circle trainers, lasers, or other devices that work but don't seem to translate easily. It is the feel that you're after, and using that feel daily will create the instinctive habits you're looking for. From time to time try also lifting the right-hand thumb completely off the grip, suspending it in the air right above the grip on plane. Switch thumbs and sometimes try even both thumbs off the club. Hitting chips and pitches like this is an eye-opening experience of how not to use the thumbs and to trust contact with this feeling.

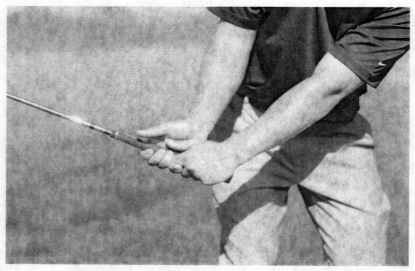

[I have had much success with this drill not only because it teaches better downswing angle and path penetration, but also because it influences *everyone's* mental game teaching *trust*.]

For your final pressure-point drill, place a piece of divot or cloth on the underside thumb knuckles as far away from the pad of the thumbs as possible. Place it in a location where you will barely be able to hold it. In this drill, the pad portion of the thumbs can be slightly lifted off the grip but the knuckle portion softly holds onto the material. This feeling of pressuring the thumbs a bit at the knuckle area only in transition will reacquaint your lag-pressure senses that just needed to be uncovered.

A good number of students have said that monitoring the pressure of the left-hand thumb knuckle was their breakthrough for consistent contact, path, and power from chips to the long game. "Talk about getting rid of the 'yips.'"

By the way, have you ever seen a golf glove that is worn so badly in the thumb pad area that it is almost shredded? Now you can understand the reason behind it; players' use these thumb pads to push the grip down toward the ground and even slide the thumb pads on the handle. This goes away with short practice using the underside of the knuckle of the thumbs wisely.

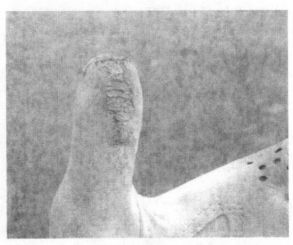

[Worn thumb pad of a new glove is quite telling.]

Next part of your daily short-game practice program is to add as many shots as you can to developing grip pressure constants. Start by monitoring a consistent three and then a four all the way to your short-game finish until you find your money pressure. In the grip-pressure practice, try varying the focus, limiting it to one area at a time such as areas of forefingers, thumbs, and even the right-hand heel pad. Your sensory focus in each different pressure point becomes less easy to recognize if you try to think of all of that at once. Eventually simplify it and find out which area seems to correlate the best solid contact and consistency. Break down your practice session even more by monitoring the pressure points for swing plane on the backswing and then the forward swing. Use a mirror as an assistant coach to view your swing plane. "Now start small and wait a few sessions before you jump into a full 7-iron shot. *** Be patient as the short game will teach you the long game if your patient.*** After several short-game sessions using these step-by-step details you will soon be able to advance all the way to your long game in every practice session. When you play the game you will have created habits which will *dramatically affect* your long game without thought. Focusing on developing these skill developments until they become habit is most important so you can play the game instinctively without how-to thoughts.

UNREFUTABLE PRINCIPLES
OF MOTION

Let's start with a gap wedge or sand wedge and set these principles in motion. Hold the golf club with a somewhat light grip pressure. Make sure that it is light enough that you have total mobility in your arms and wrists, yet still all portions of the fingers and hand pads securely on the golf club. Hold it in your left hand horizontally in front of you (see the illustration below), and move it back and forth freely cocking and uncocking your wrists. Make sure the fingers or pads of the hands are not moving around or off the club at any time.

Just this little drill alone has been a "student revelation" and must not only be understood, but also performed correctly. *It is foundational* and an absolute requirement! Most will allow the wrists to cup and flip during this little exercise. These motions will in fact destroy path, face, and clubhead speed. Learning how our wrists pronate and supinate without cupping is so very important in basic development, and it starts from the first day you pick up a golf club. For most people, the wrist's release is natural to this negative cupping during this exercise, therefore I have found it extremely valuable to teach the proper wrist/ forearm rotation from the get go. While starting with this rotation drill, make sure you rotate the wrist and forearm with the back of the left wrist remaining flat during the rotation. These motions will certainly translate with practice, so it is imperative to learn how the wrist bone pronates and supinates. Spend time here, please.

I have all my students on the forward movement try to feel the reverse position of that left wrist to a point of discomfort. This puts the wrist in an uncomfortable bowed sensation, and as you change directions from back to forward, you may have an entirely new feeling of delivery. I train this sensation even to a slight extreme because it is inherent in most people who thrust at the golf ball to have excessive cupping in the left wrist. This also can be described as a "flip" up against the left-front forearm near impact. There is a shot that we teach that requires this type of wrist release, but for this book and your development in this game, you must learn the solid basic shots first.

[This little looking flip is a big time mistake and will have huge negative ramifications in all areas of your game.]

Another important observation and feeling that you must employ is that of the right wrist. During these mini short-game movements in the backswing, you will notice that the back of the right wrist will cock back some toward the right forearm (Fig. 1). This is exactly what you're after. We want to retrain by physically holding that wrist cock during the reversing of the swing motion all the way throughout this exercise (Fig. 2 and 3). Since these are the movements of *all* great players and they cannot be refuted, it is imperative that you take a few moments in this holding drill to do them right, so they soon become habit and a normal part of your movement.

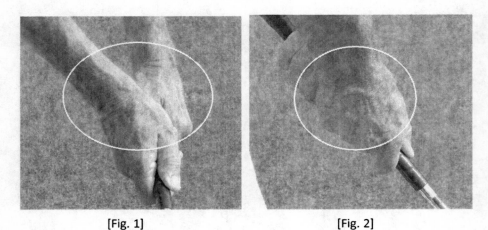

[Fig. 1]   [Fig. 2]

[Right still held in address position yet rotated through correctly.]

It would not hurt to practice this without a club in the office or while relaxing at home to make it a natural movement. One of our main drills we use in our instructional programs is to practice without the golf club, capturing the feelings of the left and right wrists positions all on correct plane lines.

[Taking the time in these shadow type swings to correct each student in each area makes this student/teacher side by side drill so very valuable. Then administering homework to master these angles, footwork, hip work, leg pressures, impact, and post-impact well before the next session accelerates development in a hurry.]

[Don't disregard these drills as they will go a long way
toward building fundamentals.]

You may already start to feel many unusual feelings that test your joints, but in all likelihood, that is a good thing. In the instruction delivery, students on this learning journey may at first feel a bit uncomfortable and maybe unorthodox (especially if they have had some previous instruction.). However these new memory movements produce shots that are dramatically improved 100 percent of the time and in astoundingly short order.

I remember as a young playing professional, many players had a self-made short weighted club that they carried around all day. They would hold it in the left hand and rotate that left wrist bone, making small swings to impact, and so on. It was considered a strengthening exercise, but more importantly, it promoted proper lever angles and rotation. I believe that many of these old timers developed their pressure points correctly without even being aware, based on feel alone to build foundational habits. How did we ever get away from such a good drill? Today we have short, cut-down clubs that some students use and hold during the day, strengthening these most important foundations to great ball striking. I prefer this pictured type of weight because players can then feel the weight at the end of the shaft. It is very hard to hold that weight if you tend to cast it a little, but if your angles and pressure points are correct then the heavy club becomes quite light. If you're a competitive player think about purchasing a small weighted club on the market to hold and make shadow swing a bit during the day. Make sure it is not so head heavy that it taxes your elbows and wrist areas to the point of possible injury.

[This old weighted club made in the garage more than thirty-five years ago has been a great tool.]

Drills for foundation acceleration:

1. With your left hand only, hold the club out in front of you parallel to the ground. Turn it to the right in a fully cocked position and then back to the left, keeping the back of your left hand dead flat and even bowed in the impact area. Do it gently and even choke up on the club if you need to at first as the club may feel quite heavy. After a few reps, bring that held club down a bit to a typical wedge plane line and repeat. You will start to recognize how the forearm bones actually rotate with the wrist. This is also one of your warm up drills each day before you practice or play you will find located at the end of the book.

2. Next do the same thing with the right hand only, but hold the cocked wrist set the entire time, back and forth. This will retrain your wrist with the new system of delivery you not only need in the short game, but in your full swings as well.

3. Soon we will advance these drills to one-handed chips and pitches that will then really advance your learning. It is fun to watch even beginners learn how to incorporate these one handers into their

practice routines. Quite amazing really to see that even in the first day of short-game instruction, they become pretty good at the drills. Translation into the long game comes surprisingly quick.

[Note the great right hand-wrist position throughout the swing of this real-time shot.]
[This will dynamically accelerate your game.]

I wanted to show the very difficult portion of the left-hand-only drill and the tendency that all of you will have at first. It is very common to have a disconnection between the left arm and the body at impact.

This was Rebecca's first time with the left-hand drill; but she was immediately able to keep the back of the left hand perfect throughout, dead flat at impact and well-held and rotated into the follow through. Note the wonderful natural and automatic movement of the body in these frames. For each of you, we need a little more connection between the arm and body, but learning what a sound left wrist and hand feel like will take your game up several levels.

CHIP-SHOT MOVEMENTS

With a good solid left-leaning format as discussed earlier in the set up, initiate the movement with the arms, hands, then shoulders, all moving in concert with each other. In the short chip shot there is no need to forcefully cock your wrists since you have a slight element of wrist cock already preset in your address position and the short distance does not require more speed. However, each player needs to know for sure the angles will increase some if your grip pressure is in a comfortable range. The golf clubhead is much heavier then the grip or the shaft; and since that is the case, this heavy head will promote the wrists to hinge load some, even on the simplest of chips. The greatest success occurs when students learn that naturally the clubhead moves/travels much further than the hands and arms since it is the end of the arc. Your job is to let it load and not hold it off. *You kill your talent and touch when you hold it off.*

[A slight natural hinge occurs if the grip pressure and pressure points are correct.] [Also note how short the arms and hands have actually moved in the backswing compared to the distance the clubhead travels. This is what you're after.]

I have always felt this is a big problem area in instruction. Learning this pendulum-type swing with *no* wrist cock is one of the stiffest and most unnatural actions one could employ, and frankly, makes no sense. As soon as you allow the heavier clubhead to swing, your wrists will cock some and produce the sweetest little contacts you can imagine.

The shoulder movements for the chip swing are similar to that of the long game just more abbreviated. They for the most part turn naturally perpendicular to your address spine angle. However many tend to take the golf club inside with their hands. This will flatten the shoulder, turn on these short chips, and reduce consistent contact and target accuracy. This is also why the pressure points and impact drills are so important. So the feeling here is the arms, hands, and then shoulders all acting as a team creating a back and through on-plane swing with natural wrist hinging. This makes distance control more predictable and achievable entirely by the length of the backswing and the loft of the club used. The clubface stays in total harmony with your turn. That is, it does not fan open more than your turn requires, nor does it close down by turning the hands under on the backswing. Simply allow the club and the clubface to travel in relationship to your connected turn.

[Connected looks of the body and arms.]

The face connection to the turn

[Connected finish looks from two angles.]

If you are feeling the shaft load a bit into your right index finger's second knuckle with thumbs and knuckles all lining up well, you will likely catch the proper face position. That being said, the face needs to naturally open as we turn so we can effectively use the built-in bounce of the club we are using. This bounce acts as a beautiful safe guard to duffed or bladed shots when returned to impact and assists the club to skid on the ground. This bounce will slide right through the grass and also prevent the infamous shut-face dig. A simple little drill for understanding this concept is to put the golf club handle in your navel and choke down to the metal shaft. Now take a simple pendulum turn and you will find that the club has an erroneous appearance of moving outside, but in reality it is only following your square to ever so slightly open setup lines. The only thing that is a bit negative of this drill is that it does not allow natural and needed hinging, so keep that in mind. The purpose here is to feel a bit of connection.

If you do set up a *hint open with your feet and your shoulders*, you will swing ever so slightly across the target line and still be on plane to your setup lines. However years of instruction have taught me all students should *at first* develop their chip and pitch techniques from a perfectly square position, aligned squarely to the target line. Note the face also as you make this connected drill as it also remains in concert with your turn without any forced closing or opening.

Over the years I have had the privilege of instructing many outstanding players that use only the sand and gap wedge for nearly every shot around the green. These players through experience have become very proficient with adjusting the loft of one or two clubs by ball position and forward shaft lean. I have no problem with this if they become extremely skilled. However even though they do not change clubs, I advocate changing lofts based on how much green one has from the fringe to the pin allowing simple easy roll out to the hole. Many greats of the game even use 4 to 5 irons to chip with from time to time. Once you learn this simple movement you will find you can adjust trajectories, spins, cuts, and roll outs at will.

THE ROLL OF THE
LEGS AND HIPS

It is not prudent to try forcing movement in the lower body in these chip shots. I believe the feet, knees, legs, and hips should move if they are in concert with the arm swing and upper body's initial athletic movement. In other words, do not hold the legs and hips from moving, but instead let them move much like they would when you gently underhand-throw a ball to someone. Some students say the look and feel of this is that everything in the upper and lower body moves sequentially together and that is not a bad thought.

Unfortunately that is not automatic for many, and even those that can toss this ball with somewhat normal weight movement do not do it very well in the full swing. This is where learning the short game movement first hugely benefits one's long game and in short order. Some people just do not move the lower half as instinctively as others, and teaching the movement here in the short shots first is the cure for that problem. Often we teachers do not spend the necessary time developing athletically challenged players and it is these players that seem to drop off and out of the game. I have found that those who we feel initially do not have the instincts of an athlete will shock you when it comes to golf. If taught in sequential order here first, I have found that these students can even become some of the finest players. I have so many that could not come close to catching a soft-tossed golf ball that became wonderful players. One in particular that I have taught won a staggering amount of tour events.

It may take a bit more time initially to learn these motions correctly, but with motivation and practice, everyone can become quite good. This little lower-body pivot and movement into a fairly fixed, slightly flexed right knee and leg is very important to great full swing ball striking. The transition of this miniature chip leg movement into the slightly taller and open left leg/hip at impact is the start of maximizing your long-game potential. This technique will also improve consistency and accuracy as well of course in these short shots. As in the full swing the left (target) side of our body acts as a strong post to hit shots against even in these little chips.

[Impact drill establishing the open taller left hip, knee, and leg at impact.]

This taller left leg, knee, and hip posted position is extremely important, also in establishing automatic release of the entire right side from top to bottom. Again as shared earlier, this is the main reason that we instruct a setup with the left leg a hint taller and slightly turned hips. It creates a mini preset impact position. Not only is the face of the club affected by proper use of the lower body, but also the delivery of all the power sources are as well. These little movements in my opinion cannot be learned in the long game easily. This is the reason most *learn the game backwards*. You will accelerate your development, exponentially learning productive impact in these small chips first before bringing them naturally into your long game. This makes the foundational building of these small chips and pitches *extremely* important.

Now allowing the lower body its athletic travel nature, start these little shots by again allowing this slight weight change and pivot into a well-held right knee flex as well as an unchanging entire right-leg angle. That right leg and hip may naturally receive a little weight, but actually do not change their address lean angle.

[In this pitch shot the right leg and hip receive a bit of weight but hold their original address angle and right-knee flex. The left leg and hip are the pivot points.]

If you change that angle much, you will struggle to move back to the left side with decent timing as the swing gets longer in pitches and shots. I always share with students that as the chip swing increases in size, the athletic instinctive movement of the left knee will move a bit more toward that right leg in the backswing. For some nonathletic folks, I spend extra time here establishing this tiny movement, so it very quickly will become instinctive. I will not move on until they get the *Aha!* moment and can repeat it easily.

Next in the forward-chip swing, the legs need to move back into the tiny posted-up left hip, knee, and leg. These miniature movements of the legs are the foundational precursor to everything you do in your long game. So learn diligently how to post up into a miniature swing impact position, and hold it until the ball stops rolling. The purpose for the hold is to help train the brain to recognize proper movements, balance, and distance-feel controls; which eventually makes the entire sequence automatic. Plus this held finish plays a role in the development of your mental game, believe it or not. Since developing your mental game in each practice is paramount to your playing well in pressure circumstances, holding will add confidence *and* create great habits. Without smart habits, you will almost always revert to what is habit even in the smallest pressure situations. If your "DNA," as I call it, or what you have made a habit is not a well-established good habit then it is what you will get in these moments of pressure.

"THE PELVIC TRIANGLE"

Years of research and student development have shown me that few understand how the hips actually move and hold in golf. One of the cornerstones of my instruction career in shot making and total game development has been the role of the pelvis and hip sockets or ASIS joints. Proper movements are easily learned in the short game area but truthfully *nearly impossible* to learn in the longer game. Without it, every single student will never reach his or her God-given ball-striking potential. It is groundbreaking and imperative to great ball striking. It is not difficult to learn and then incorporate into the full swing if we start small and then work forward. I personally believe that possible professional careers have been dead-ended early because of this lack of understanding. Let's revisit how we set our hips earlier with bending from the hip/pelvis area and not from the stomach and or back. Start by standing straight up, feet about the width of a short-game shot, with a slight knee bend only. Place your forefingers once again in the front hip socket areas as shown below to capture the proper pelvis bending.

Next bend at the hip area, only keeping the back perfectly flat as you bend into a typical posture. When you feel this reset of the pelvis and hips into the athletic posture spoken of earlier, you will have felt the flex that is to remain throughout the chip, pitch, and full swing for that matter. Now move into your right side without a club in a shadow type of chip or pitch motion.

Feel once again how the right and the left hip flexors have moved. If you feel the preset at address changed any at all in either hip, regardless of the hip turn, you have moved your pelvis incorrectly; and it will guarantee the need of many compensations to hit even a simple chip. *Nearly 100 percent* of all golfers lose *not only* the left hip flex angle early in the backswing, but also lose even more dramatically the right hip flex angle on the forward swing. This improper motion basically creates a new person who addresses the ball closer than the former position that they started with. Clearly as your body is in an entirely different position, your body will have to act differently and compensate to make decent contact. As the swing gets a bit larger, it negatively changes more dramatically, requiring even more compensatory moves to hit shots. This foundational principle is missed by many players and teachers and causes everyone to miss potential. It is really difficult to learn in the long game straight away and must first be understood and practiced with small motions until it is developed correctly.

[But the good news is everyone can learn it.]

At transition or the change of directions, I have found that same percentage of all golfers again lose the angles spoken of even more dramatically. Not only do many relocate that left-hip address position, but they also move that now-scooted forward pelvic region well toward the ball on the forward motion. The foundation of your address set of your hips now is actually many inches forward and toward the ball. This is true even if you have tried in vain to hit shots against the taller-posted target leg. You can imagine what happens to players now as they drift their hips forward, depleting the player of the necessary room for the delivery to impact. Arms and hands become trapped on the full swing and also on these short little chips and pitches.

Now I do not want this to seem complicated so I want to go over how I teach it with words, drills, and pictures so you can easily learn it. Years on the lesson tee have taught me that everyone needs to start this training in the short game first and master it there before you go to half-swing shots and beyond.

To capture the feelings of the correct hip work, I will get behind the student and put my hands in their hip sockets at address then assist them during the turn into the backswing.

[In these sequences I am physically holding these hip joints
from scooting forward toward the ball.]

Invariably the hips will try to change their flex angle that they had at address and scoot the stomach/rear toward the ball. I then hold those positions, not allowing this scoot, and it feels weird to students. The same happens on the forward swing, and when approaching impact, I hold that hip flex area so they can move into impact with the hip flex from both sides intact.

This Foundational Principle must be taken care of. You miss it, and you miss your talent.

Great drills for pelvic foundation.

1. Shadow moves with your fingers set against the front side of your hips, locating that tilt and maintaining that tilt throughout to chip and pitch finish.

2. Hips slightly backed into a wall behind you. Back in, and do not lean into that wall but barely graze it. You can easily do the same thing with a couple shafts covered with foam material as shown to create a more defined feel. Place one behind each hip so that you are barely touching them at address. In your swing then, feel that touch gently grazing throughout.

With a wedge in hand, move into that solid right side while at the same time just slightly still maintain that right-hip touch against the shaft or wall. It is likely that the left hip may come off the wall or shaft a tiny bit as you turn some, but it is a good to practice with both hips slightly touching in these small chip shots. Moving into the forward swing, the right hip will only slightly come off the wall, but the left will return to its address touch and maybe even more dramatically be touching at impact and post-impact. Another good feeling can be to sense your *tail bone* remaining intact as you move right and then left to deliver impact.

3.   Next drill, put a small ball between your knees to train your hips and legs how to turn and move in these little chips. As the chip becomes a pitch requiring your feet to be incrementally further apart, use a bit larger ball to balance out your feet and knee width.

4. For years I have used *balloons* when teaching away from my home
    facility. The balloon is such a good tool since it is so pliable and
    adjustable. The different sizes and shapes come in handy for just
    tons of drills in all areas of the game. Note on this drill that the
    balls/balloon position must not slide out of position or slide into
    a different location on your knees as you move. This will not only
    require you to maintain your pelvis in both directions, but will also
    teach and demonstrate how the right knee and feet move in a
    good forward chip and pitch. At the end of this book you will find a
    part of your morning routine that will advance your development
    in this area.

[If the ball comes out on these little shots, you have likely lost the right hip joint.]

Also place the two shafts behind you while using the ball to practice staying in your original address position throughout the swing. The old single shaft behind your left hip drill is not good enough, as it still will allow your right hip to negatively scoot well toward the ball, giving you the false impression that you're doing the drill well and making progress.

[Even in the backswing as you pivot into the right side, the left hip should be very near its original flex and hold location in these short shots.]

5. Final drill here for now is to have someone locate a shaft just an
    inch or so in front of your stomach/thighs as you practice this
    move.

During the movement you may not touch the shaft in any direction.
You can even hit little chip shots completing this drill, making it
all-important, real-time practice.

THE CHIP HOLD

From the original set position of your shaft lean and preset right-and-left-wrist set, it is imperative to maintain that position all the way to post-impact. Most allow the left wrist to cup and the right wrist to roll under. If the right hand rolls under, the clubhead will pass the hands, also known as the flip, which results in fat and thin shots. The hold-by description is actually maintaining the left-and-right-wrist address positions along with address shaft lean into impact and beyond. If accomplished, players then require only the length of the swing and the loft of the club to determine distances of the chip shot.

The feel that you're after is to be able to create that hold with only pressure point focus. It is important to not grip the club tight and strangle the handle. Remember the tension and pressure point drills we discussed earlier? Find your comfortable number in the three-to-five range and use it here as well. Allow the hands and forearms to properly rotate all connected in correlation with the body's rotation. The clubhead will arrive to impact much later since it is at the bottom of the arc. This also means as the upper and lower body turn open post impact, you will have the feeling that you're moving the arms and club around to the left but yet still in front of your turning body.

[Well-held tension-free, solid, small-pitch position)

Many students mistakenly tend to overextend their arms toward the target well away from their body to keep the hands from cupping pre-impact and beyond.

[This is an unnatural mistake and must be corrected.]

It is very important that properly connected foundational movement between the body and the golf club is *understood* before you move on. I have had great results with having all students hold their connected chip finish well-balanced on their left-posted leg until after the ball lands. This way they can check their finish positions and also monitor their pressure points and tension levels. This type of feedback is *very important* to accelerating your ability to master distance and full-swing development through these short game principles. Now there are tons of drills and teaching aids that assist those who just struggle so much with these angle holds. We have had a few students that may have struggled for a moment but never ever had any that did not get it and be able to use it for the rest of their lives. My advice in this area is to work at it and don't move on until you have learned it instinctively and "habitually." Once you have it and you make it habit, it will transfer into the subconscious mind for use in pressure situations on the golf course. This is why we have the student-teacher interview process for each student before we ever start our journey together. There are a few concepts that are absolutely necessary to improve and will indeed lead to great enjoyment, therefore we should both agree to not budge until these are well-learned. Take the time to master these things, and then each and every practice session will *forever* routinely include these foundational principles at least in your warm-up. Build great habits in these short-game shots so you can instinctively *trust* them in the heat of competition.

Drills

1. First try chips with your pitching wedge, chocking down enough on the club that you have plenty of grip out the end of your hands for this *grip drill*. That hidden grip at address must be hidden at least at impact and not show itself between your arms. The handle end of that grip needs to be located the same distance from your stomach post-impact as it was at address as well in the connected chip/pitch motion. Look at the following illustrations:

[Grip end is still connected and hidden nicely just after real time impact.]

2. Another favorite of mine is to have your practice partner hold his grip end of the shaft just twelve to eighteen inches past impact just away from the post impact proper plane line. Your job is to hit

that chip and not make contact with their shaft. Positioning that correctly located instruction shaft post-impact will take care of improper, exaggerated overextension as well.

[You can also position this shaft in such a way that it will assist with connection from address to finish.]

3. Another is the hit and stop all with proper grip pressure and pressure points. The hands and wrists are to stop as near impact as possible with the hands well in front of the clubhead. It feels sort of like a punch stop with the hands and wrists in the premium positions that have been referred to earlier. The stop drill as I call it, has reformed many a student.

[The Stop Drill.]

4. Another is to place a bench or stool in front of the student and have them chip their ball low enough under the stool but not allow the shaft or clubhead to make contact. The idea here is to capture this new feeling, and then through practice make it instinctively soft and habit.

5. Another drill that all students should use every practice session is the right-hand-only chip. Seems a bit hard at first, but in just short order, students find the necessary body-and-arm-connected movement easily, holding this connection into post-impact.

It is here that one feels the natural cocking and the simple softness of the shot with the finish-wrist position still held in its original wrist flex. This is the same flex that is established at address and in the backswing. It is surprising to all first timers how easily the ball is crisply hit with little or no effort as long as the focus is in the wrist and also pressure points. By the way you can also use this same drill in the bunker with surprising easy results.

6. Practice the same drill now with the left hand, which to nearly every first timer is much harder. The idea of this little chip drill of course is to learn the natural hinging of that left hand on the backswing and to deliver to impact without even a glimpse of flip. It is then that students start to realize that these little shots are moved more with the arms and the body then they actually are with the hands.

[May be hard but should be part of every single practice session.]

7. Finally one of my favorites has been the extra long, fifty-two-degree driver length, double-gripped wedge that extends well beyond the regular grip for chip and long-game work. As pictured below, that long, extended handle needs to stay in front of the arms yet connected (in space) to the body's original setup and rotation during the movement and finish.

This is a practice club everyone can make themselves, and also one that will simply make you a much better player. Also nice to have that type of club in an 8-iron loft with a very strong shaft to practice in the long game full swings. This extra long club helps everyone learn valuable release and rotation concepts.

Holding Reminder:

Just the word *hold* as used in the title of this chapter tends, however, to signal the incorrect mental picture. Many associate this word with tightness and feel that they need to tighten the hands and arms in order to keep the clubhead from passing the hands. Squeezing the club tight to eliminate wrist flip is not the answer, although it is in the beginning the feeling for most. Once you understand the feelings of the arm-and-body-generated swing, you will be able to hit your chips even with light pressure and maintain a comfortable hold.

PACE, RHYTHM, AND TIMING

I believe that nearly every person misunderstands unique pace and rhythm in the context of the golf swing and mental applications. Our job as teachers is to help each person find their unique personal rhythm and pace, which will greatly assist them locating their timing sequences.

Pace is typically dictated by your personality and even a bit by each player's blood type in my opinion. An A type typically approaches life a little more hasty and driven than an O or B type, and so on. Not always the case, but it is a good starting point for me in establishing student's pace. It doesn't do a lot of good to be a Greg Norman-driven type of personality trying to swing like a Fred Couples type, although it is true that these two professionals have paces that are much closer than one would think. Typically this person would always be working on slowing down the engine. Just trying each day to slow your swing and tempo down is very difficult to say the least and will likely bite you on the golf course.

Additionally we also use the DISC system of personality management to help students recognize their type of general personality, but for the sake of this simple book we will spare these details. If you like, you can simply Google *disc* and get to a sight to read about this important information or go to my favorite sight: http://www.mentalgolfworkshop.com/.

To get a decent understanding of each student, I have them walk their normal walk twenty-five yards away from and then back to me to assist me determining their pace of the swing and their rhythm walk. I also like to have those that are competing in events where they must carry their own bag walk with their bag at exactly their normal type of pace.

With metronome as shown in hand we can pretty much determine what each player's natural pacing should be and compare that to the chips and pitches they are showing me.

Two additional drills we have incorporated in our schools are two types of arm-swing rhythms to determine pace. Naturally swinging the arms from side to side and then up to down creates for us a general consistent pace of the long game and the short game for each player. We can then tune our metronomes to these same rhythm beats or find correlating music to listen to.

As you can see in the pictures the metronome is in front of us on the ground. We adjust the student's metronome to match their *natural* and comfortable arm swinging motion backward and forward, which then easily translates into their beating system for their short-game shots.

Once the natural arm-swinging knowledge and their rhythm walk is understood, then each student's rhythm and pace is established in the short game (For the long game there are additional needed adjustments due to the length of the swing.). We can share simple beating sounds (that match the metronome) that they may be able to hum, set their typical iPod music to, or even hear with several possible metronome unique sounds used in the schools. Once it starts to feel very good then we can come back to it any time that our timing and rhythm feels off. Your key is to *monitor* your pace and learn your tendencies, such as hurrying the shot outside of your step flow, grabbing the club, or perhaps throwing portions of your body at the golf ball to get it to the hole, and so on. The pace and rhythm is dictated by the bigger muscles of the upper body, shoulders, and arms and not the thrash of the hands.

Pay close attention to this. For timing purposes, we also focus mastering rhythm in the lower body's arrival time. Since many players are typically overzealous and early with the legs and hips, the metronome is such a valuable resource drill of timing as well. Initially teaching these arrival principles in the short game first really helps players grow their personal rhythm in the long game. Listen to this statement from this long-time instructor:

> If you are taught basic rhythm-body delivery principles in the short-game first and spend some good quality time there practicing that delivery rhythm, you will *not* struggle with overzealous hips and legs that run away from you on the forward swing of the long game.

That is a big statement but a fact for sure with every student that I have worked with. So all of you reading this that have overzealous delivery sequences of your legs and hips, and literally millions do, you finally have a plan of how to take care of that now. The wonderful thing about this timing instruction is you don't ever have to say slow down legs or speed up arms and a myriad of other horrible thoughts in a practice session.

Educating the consistent acceleration principles of body, hand, and wrist delivery using the metronome has been a critical component of my instruction. When students realize early in session one that the arm-and-hand delivery is a simple type of personal and natural flow, they can easily take this right into their larger type of pitch shots. It is actually quite fun to watch.

There are several mental factors here which I introduce right from the start. If you're this far in this book, you deserve to hear at least one of these truths of "flow." Your body has a beautiful internal-beating system created from the beginning of our existence. This rhythm is a three—and a four-part beat that nearly everyone misunderstands. In my studies of human performance and flow, I have found that many people move about in their everyday lives in a two-beat stressed type of flow. I have noticed this a lot in many of the Asian countries that I teach in. Many things are done on a one-two beat. The walk is a one-two, the language is a one-two, and so on. For you golf flow is not performed as well in this one-two type of flow. The tendency is to be way too static and quick, of course. Europeans, Americans, and many other societies typically do most things on a three-beat system, but the average amateur does not employ this system in general sports. The simple reason behind this is that they lack the understanding of physical and mental flow. All our measurements taken over the many years of instruction show that the greats of the game employ a three-beat flow in the short game and putting and a four-beat type of flow in the long game. Through countless hours of experimentation and study, we have found for the short game near perfect success with typical two beats on the backswing and a gentle return of one beat on the forward swing to impact. The first of those beats is the signal to start, the second is the final backswing location, and the final beat is impact. That is, for the legs, arms, and shoulders, all arriving *on rhythm*.

If you were counting it out you would count 1=start, 2=completion of the backswing, and 3=impact arrival with all body parts lining up at precisely the same time.

For the long game we use a four-beat motion due to the length of the swing. There are three beats used from start to the top completed position and one during the forward motion to impact. These rhythm cycles have proven 100 percent of the time to be extremely effective and produce some of the finest shots you may ever encounter. Not only will you produce better leverage resulting in more consistent and penetrating contact, but you will also affect your mental game as you focus on your flow rather than mechanics and outside distractions. What is really cool about these ten years of testing regarding body vibrations and metronome-rhythm characteristics is that testing with a launch monitor gave us all the proof we needed. In *every single case* that clubhead speed, ball speed, face angle, and path were dramatically improved immediately in thousands of amateur and professional players we tested. Not only in golf, but in many other major sports and occupations, the results continue to be amazing. There is so much more for those of you out there that want to play the game at the highest levels possible using these field-flow principles. Understanding these flow dimensions of mental balance, performance, and creating positive energy balance in sports has been researched and proven time and again. Takashi Ohara, my great friend and I have studied field flow-driven positive energy taking the art of quantified simpler mental performance to a much higher level for students. The great part about instructing this *harmony flow* is that it is not abstract but easy to wrap your arms around in a concrete way. These simple and basic rhythm and pacing techniques that we have put together for the high performance athlete have created a personal practical way of developing "flow" at will. You will see more on this in the future. For you in this book, let's leave this area with just a good solid understanding of the body's internal pace and beat system and practice it diligently.

Drills

For smart drill, get yourself a simple "guitar" metronome that has possible multiple pitch and time settings. Set your short-game training metronome to a generic three-quarters time at 84-90 beats to the minute. Since this is, in my opinion, a fairly moderate to quick pace, you may decide to adjust this number a bit lower to find your own natural flow. If you're an O blood type start with eighty-four, if a B, maybe an eighty-seven, and an A may begin right at ninety. These are initial possible starting points and are not set in concrete.

Start your chip-type swing on that first beat which could be a higher-pitch sound if you have that type of metronome. The second beat should find your backswing completed.

That third and final beat *must* find the lower body, upper torso, arms, hands, and club all arriving right on time to the perfect impact-loaded position discussed earlier.

Moving this into the larger pitches as well accelerates student understanding and learning. This pace flow is a lot easier to understand if students monitor the pressure points rather than trying to slow something. This focused attention on the points will assist you a lot as you attempt to only deliver these points rather than the clubhead.

Another very important drill, especially for those that tend to have their lower bodies outrace the arms in their long game, is focusing your pace beats in the lower body only. Focus on having your lower body in a powerful impact position, in perfect sequence with the beats. The beautiful purpose of this drill is to not allow your hips and legs to zealously arrive way too early with arms and hands lagging behind as countless players do especially in the long game, trapping themselves at impact. Also for some who do not do a good job of even getting to the strong left side at impact, this drill works extremely well for you. Players can then easily see how this then will translate into the full shots, establishing the finest rhythm, pace, and timing you have ever experienced.

One of my favorite drills of all time is the right-arm swing only. Monitoring pace and delivery techniques of that right on-plane forearm with all points intact is a big surprise to many. It is quite easy after a few shots to hit such crisp chips and pitches with great flow.

Another drill is to hit shots off the chipping green putting surface (around the edges, please.) Contact after pure contact in flow is a great motivator as everyone agrees that hitting such crisp effortless shots from this dicey location promotes the necessity for *huge trust*.

Again let me reiterate a bit about your pace walk on the golf course and in all of life for that matter. This personality walk that puts you in a nice-flowing type of unhurried rhythm is exactly what you want on the course. In your competitive rounds, the way you walk and the way you move not only with your legs and arms, but also your eyes dramatically effects *zone* possibilities. Monitoring your established pace while you play using your beating system and even matching personalized music will go a *long* way toward better play. The reasons are obvious as nearly every player who seems to play that outstanding tournament or round of golf shares that things were easier and they felt like they could see things better. Most players who have not experienced this would say, "Well, what is that, and how do I order it?" It is a practiced flow complete with rhythm thoughts, gentle clarity, eye monitoring, walk pacing, harmony, skilled habits, and trust.

THE PITCH AND HOLD MOTION

The pitch setup is a little different of course then the simple straight-forward chip. First due to the longer shot we need a little wider foundation to support the size of the swing. So as needed based on the size of the swing, incrementally widen your feet more to support your backswing length and good balance on the insides of your feet. Next as your swing gets a little larger you will need to adjust the setup distance a bit further from the ball. Since we are all unique, it will require a bit of experimenting with gradually moving a little further away as your need for distance increases. A good starting point here is the hand-and-arm gravity hang right below the shoulders.

The basic first-ball position near middle to slightly back of middle with the shaft not nearly as far pressed forward as the typical chip shot. Just like the chip however, weight distribution should favor the target side leg and hip. A good start once again is a 60/40 percent relationship.

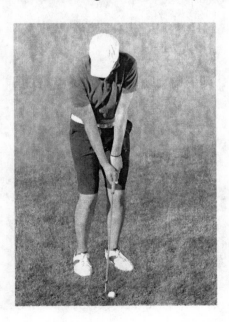

In the case of the simple pitch, we desire to involve the bounce of the club as much as possible and to do that your basic shaft-leaning position needs to be much less forward pressed. Just a simple near-straight line from the left shoulder to the clubhead will suffice for most. Coupling that with the new near middle-ball position, the bounce of the golf club will be encouraged.

The pitch requires us (due to the length of the shot) to allow for a bit more angle set. I say allow, as I think it best not to have to force set your wrists but just allow natural instincts and clubhead weight to intuitively create the set. The hands and body can adequately take care of the wrist set on the backswing, but we sure do need angles to assist with distance and pure contact. The clubface stays in concert with your turn into the backswing opening only to the extent of your turn. If you swing the club back about one-third of the way and pause when the shaft is near parallel to the ground, the toe should be pointing near straight up in a square clubface position. If you start with a slightly open face at address then that square face will look a bit more open in the backswing.

[The clubface is not forced closed by an under rotating of the wrists nor opened by a fanning of the wrists but is in direct relationship to the turn and wrist set.]

The legs will now start to instinctively desire to become more active due to the length of the backswing. Allow your left knee and your weight to move into the right side as needed and pulled there by your arm swing and the upper body's movement. Just like that little chip however, you're still establishing the left leg and hip area as your pivot post. The right will receive a little weight, but it also continues to act as a set flexed post to turn against, exactly the same as the chip albeit with a bit more hip turn (due to the size of the swing).

[Weight still on the left side even at the final location of the backswing makes it a lot easier to post well into the left side at impact.]

Planes and Hinging

To capture a good understanding of correct wrist hinging, I have found it very helpful to start with this simple drill early on. You also may find this beneficial. With a good pliable but solid 4-grip pressure, assume a square pitch-type address. Now stand up and hold the club and arms horizontally directly in front of you. Cock the club naturally to vertical without a change in grip pressure yet all components of fingers and hands on the club. Note the natural set of both the left and right wrists and how that vertical shaft feels when loaded straight up. This bit of cocking in both wrists is a perfectly natural action and needs to be gradually permitted and promoted. Note and feel the weight of the club and its location in the hands and fingers as the wrists hinge. Continue this drill until it starts to feel quite natural.

Next advance this drill exaggerating the hinging up and down from a normal address plane line a third of the way into the swing as shown in the pictures. These two drills will promote how the hinge really works and the pressure locations of the fingers and wrists.

As the pitch swing naturally becomes progressively longer based on needed distances, the angle set becomes more naturally pronounced. This angle hinge needs to produce a shaft and hands that continuously ride the correct path on the backswing. This is similar to the simple chip; the golf club, arms, and hands need to stay in front of our chest as we turn this pitch swing a little deeper in the backswing.

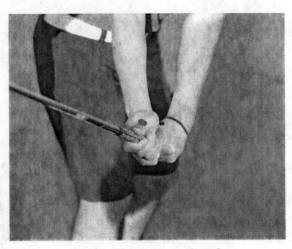

[All components on plane.]

Golfers tend to permit the clubhead, hands, and the shaft to travel way inside during the initial backswing, creating a flat trapped early start of the swing. Adding to that is the tendency to fan open the clubface which adds another dicey ingredient to the mix.

[It is not unusual to see clubhead, hands and arms traveling inside like this.]

This mistaken position then forces *everyone* to make several needed compensatory movements to hit a decent shot. The first of which is to create the necessary room so the arms do not get completely trapped behind the body. The trap position forces players to create an outside downswing and a very steep approach to at least make contact.

[Outside around and cutting across.]

This of course causes the pull, cut, and weak-type shots as the club, hands, and arms come completely across the target line. Along with that poor path, the task of getting to the ball becomes extremely difficult as you will need a wrist cast to *even* make contact.

Poor long-swing movements that many have developed are tough habits to break the conventional way.

Drills

Adding an umbrella or shaft stuck in the ground a few inches outside the middle of your right foot and another shaft that mirrors the address plane line located just barely out of reach on the backswing are effective ways of promoting *visual* path understanding.

Additional simple tools, such as an extra long tee pressed into the end of the grip and the driver-length wedge as shown, are great visualization drills. One of our student's all-time favorites has been adding an additional shaft to the grip that points and almost touches the target line on both the backswing and forward swing.

Another drill, if you have the opportunity to practice indoors, is a reasonably priced laser attached to the end of your grip. Feedback from the lazer as you move throughout your pitch is a valuable indoor tool.

Another way of feeling the connected backswing path and face is by pressing the grip end of a golf club into your navel, choking down on the club to the shaft, and turning. You will not only notice how the face naturally opens with the turn-in relation to your spine angle, but you will also see as you cock your wrists that extended handle pointed directly at the target line.

TRANSITION

It has been well documented that effective transition separates good players from great players. An efficient transition plays a major role in the swing and seems to be a shot in the dark for the average player. At transition, as the forward swing begins, players tend to bring extremely weakened angles to the golf ball for many misunderstood reasons. Therefore it is one of the most important concepts to understand and learn right from the beginning. My experience has taught me that the best way to understand effective transitioning is through principles of the short game. I believe it is rarely possible to learn proper transition any other way and I bet many of you reading this will attest to that fact as you have likely spent countless hours trying to achieve better delivery angles.

In the full swing of most decent ball strikers, a near-ninety-degree angle between the left arm and the shaft is formed two-thirds of the way into the backswing (Not everyone, but most players.). These angles increase in depth immediately at transition, building a powerful loaded force to deliver to the golf ball. The angle becomes even more dramatic a bit further into the downswing, building even more leverage. All great ball strikers have acquired this technique while the average player struggles to find it.

[Larger angle even this late in the swing must be learned
in fundamental short shots first.]

Increased angles result from natural forces that are available to every human being playing this great game but remain so elusive that people spend lifetimes trying to find it. That is unfortunate because if you learn these transitions in short swings first, you're likely to advance toward hitting the tightest golf shots you have ever hit without having to deal with angles.

For more than twenty-five years I have filmed many students hitting their typical casted-iron shots and also taped them throwing golf clubs forty yards or more to a target. This was done without instruction and 100 percent of the time these videos show better balance, stronger angles, improved leg positions at impact, and more. Why on earth is that? The brain knows that if you release early and cast the club from the top, you will stick your clubhead into the ground. In the case of throwing the club to the target, everyone, after a few tries, instinctively and athletically holds that angle until well after impact. With a few more tries we had found that it became natural and thoughtless. Interesting and 100 percent full proof for athletic players and nonathletic as well (Now do not do this without some supervision as those first few throws can travel many surprising and dangerous places!). For many years I carried a tennis racket and Wiffle ball bat in my instruction bag. I would sit on a stool and toss Wiffle balls up in the air and have students hit these with both the racket and the bat all on video.

[These angles are very common even for less-skilled players.]

Swinging at a ball tossed in the air shows near-perfect angles in transition. I then tried the same thing with a 6 iron in hand and tossed the Wiffle ball again; results were still nearly perfect. However when that ball is motionless on the ground, most have the desire (and misconception) to hit at it. Tee that same ball up on a t-ball tee similar to the pictures below and hit a 6-iron shot at baseball height, and students all achieve the same great results.

1.   2.   3.

4.   5.   6.

[Note the angle change and right elbows natural drop that automatically comes from the takeaway in picture number three to the forward swing in picture number five. This happens in every single case for every player when the ball is teed up at this height.]

Note also the perfect leg work and balance that almost all players instinctively execute.

The point of this little diversion is to share with you that everyone reading this book can become a much better ball striker using simple concepts with new understanding starting *very small* and working toward *big*.

To begin to understand the transition process, we must start by understanding the angles of the forward motion.

Starting with a light 4-grip pressure on the takeaway, you will see in the forward swing how the angle increases even in a small-chip and pitch shot provided you continue your consistent grip pressure. This is really important, as many players subconsciously fear the golf ball and since their goal is to deliver the clubhead to hit the golf ball and get it airborne, they increase the grab of the club. Grabbing will always change and adjust angles in the swing, resulting in a casting motion in order to make decent contact. We can see this in close-up videos as students grab with fingers and thumbs in their effort to change directions quickly to hit their shots. This of course will result in many inconsistencies and loss of power. The trouble is that you have heard and read all this before. The difference is now we seek to give you a good understanding of what actually takes place and a quantified way to make it happen for you.

For drill, maintain the same grip pressure and hold the club about two feet off the ground. Begin by moving your arms, hands, and golf club back and forth together a short distance, practicing this transition movement. I want you to feel how your wrists hinge naturally and then the angle increases as you softly move from the backswing toward impact position.

[Note the slight transition angle change
in Fig. 2 as the arms initiate the forward sequences.]

Make sure that your movements are clean by not allowing your grip to slide around or come off the club. You are simply allowing the club to move in its normal pattern and almost gravity drop as I say into the forward swing. You can now feel the transition angles change some to a deeper angle. Add your light pressure points and especially feel the added pressure of the right palm against the left thumb as you move these points toward the impact area. Experiment with the different pressure points discussed in the chip chapters and monitor these points, finding the ones that seem to work best for you. You will soon be using these pressure points and grip pressure in the full swing also.

Our emphasis here is that you are feeling the clubhead as your arms initiate forward swing delivery and your weight shifts from the takeaway to the forward swing, and then back to impact position. As it becomes more comfortable and instinctive, you will quickly lose the tightening of the wrists, pushing of the thumbs, and grabbing of the fingers that plague so many players.

THE POST-IMPACT HOLD

Every single player that is a strong ball striker has more forward shaft lean at impact then they do at address. The short game is no different. If you could catch a camera close-up of the typical tournament players' clubhead near impact, you would note that the loft is much less then it was at address. Often with extremely high-level video equipment we note the driver just previous to impact continues to de-loft. This late pre-impact de-loft is what the hold really is. These players are in a different position at impact than they were at address and you should as well. This is incredible and monumental to great ball striking. Now we realize that many of you reading this book do not have the time to devote to the game as these players do *but* there is no reason you can't learn de-lofting techniques and impact holds as a casual or even light competitive player.

[Impact is well forward of original circled address
in this live fifteen-yard pitch shot.]

You will also note that the shaft has a forward lean to it toward the target and may even have a little bow in it on full-swing shots.

[Full swing 6 iron that also looks effortless.]

It does not mean that advanced players are stronger than you are and that you can't create speed as well with little effort. On the contrary 100-pound juniors can generate some serious clubhead speed moving tee shots more than 250 yards.

[Alexis at age 13]

This of course effectively changes the loft of the club and they now are hitting one club more then they started with, i.e. a 6 iron, two hundred yards. Now you have it. Actually a few of the students that I teach tend to de-loft almost too much, and we have to back up and deliver with less angles so the ball will have some decent trajectory. Nearly all amateur players would love to have this problem. Impact also finds the back of the target hand facing the target and as post-impact continues in the full swing, that impact is held for a very brief microsecond, creating what I term as a "long flat spot." This hold creates penetrating laser-type shots even with your wedges.

This is the hold. It is not a purposeful hold but it becomes a distinctive automatic intuitive hold briefly and then a correct connected natural rotation as the swing continues into the finish side of the swing.

Major Drill

So again let's get started with a sand wedge pitch-type set up. Address your standard bread-and-butter position without a ball at first in front of a mirror for immediate feedback. Make a pitch-size rehearsal swing to impact. Note the more forward position of your de-lofted clubface and the dead flat even bowed position of the left hand.

Again feel the transition reloading of the angle and try stopping at impact. Do it slowly enough that you can easily stop. Now hold that body connected position as you move a little past impact. The feel and look here is a nice shoulder and arm triangle that was originally set up at address continues to impact. Again this triangle will be a bit more forward toward the target in the impact location, including wrists, hands, and shaft angle as shown.

[Address triangle in black; live impact in white.]

This will feel a little foreign to you, but proceed and see if it does not get easier. At first I will not let my students hit balls until I am pretty sure they have the concept and can feel the difference between the correct feel and the opposite tendency to flip the hands and clubhead under the ball. Upon introducing the ball now some students will still flip the left wrist, allowing the clubhead to pass up the hands a bit, breaking down the triangle delivery. Now the oh-I-get-it moment arrives for nearly everyone with each realizing their tendency to hit at the ball. From here progress happens quickly, and each little chip and pitch start having that unique crisp impact sound with the bounce of the club being utilized. I want the hold post-impact mastered on these little chips and pitches and for the student to stop and hold this little finish position so they can take inventory.

[Post-impact still well-held connected position.]

Once students have this in the first short-game lesson, I immediately have them hit these little chip-type shots off our practice pitching green. At first they are a little freaked out with the worry hitting balls off the pitching green, but after two to three shots they can pinch that ball right off the surface and the contact after impact on the surface does not damage the green. Listen these are not all strong players, but some have handicaps of 20-30, men, women, and children. It becomes so darn easy. The hardest part of this is sharing it in written word. Beginners get a great start learning this way as it circumvents rebuilding all the poor fundamentals. We have professional golfers from several countries come and relearn some of these principles and leave much better ball strikers. I am of the firm belief that due to improper practice and learning, there are many players out there that could have been tremendous ball strikers and scorers of the ball yet have fallen short because of improper practice and basic block-building skills. I have found that after a few weeks of practice, every student, regardless of level, can hit their chips and pitches with much more confidence, leverage, and control.

TODAY'S MODERN FITTING

In today's technology of golf equipment and our new industry of well-trained understanding of personalized fitting, it is really a sizable mistake not to have equipment in our hands that assists contact and spin consistency. Even the casual player needs to at least have the correct lie angle and effective bounce on the wedges. Without spending a lot of time here suffices it to say the following. At impact in your short chips and pitches, it is important that the toe of the golf club is on the ground so the heel doesn't drag. Heel dragging will cause the toe to close down at impact and will result in pulls, poor contact and poor trajectory. This will be even more dramatic in lies in longer grass. In addition, the bounce on your club is there for good reason and that is to create less digging of the leading edge providing a nice little skid along the turf. This is due to the trail edge of the sole being a bit deeper then the lead edge, creating the skid contact on the ground.

(Note 10 degrees of bounce lifts the leading edge well
off the surface at normal address)

This is such a good feeling, creating not only much better contact, but also more consistency in spin. The great thing about this is you do not always have to spend more money to purchase new wedges, but you can have your lie angles bent and adjusted at a local golf shop. If you don't take the time to bend correctly, your equipment will not match your impact tendencies, then you will be forced to create necessary compensations to make decent impact. These compensations will make their way right into your long game, truly defeating the purpose of the chapters you have just read.

Try this at home. Add a strip of electrician's tape to the bottom of your wedge soles and hit a few short pitch shots or just make short pitch contacts for that matter on a hard surface such as the garage floor. Note the marks after several 15-yard-type pitch swings. If the tape contact is in the middle of the sole in the bounce area, then you're likely in business with your lie angle and bounce degrees. But if it is slightly off in different locations, then you certainly need adjustments. It costs very little to take care of this and you will see immediate results. In the bounce department, a correct amount of bounce for many may again assist in club skid through impact rather than dig, so experiment with different degrees of bounce as well. Please spend some time with your local well-trained PGA professional to check these important necessities.

TRANSITIONING TO LONGER SHOTS

It is important to not jump right into the full swing immediately but take the foundation building one step at a time from the short-game chips and pitches to the half-swing wedges. Remember in our programs we have at least three to six 90-minute, short-game sessions with all students first before we start into the long game. Even after all these developmental sessions are completed, the assigned homework for the motivated student is always to spend thirty minutes minimum of each practice session going over the mentioned short-game points for the appropriate lead into your long-game practices. Your job is to build your own practice formula that seems to cement and promote your new foundation. Make this a part of your warm-ups and pre-round practice program, developing new *habits* that will soon become intuitive.

Transitioning into longer shots is where the fun begins. I would say about 90 percent of the time each student will progress rapidly enough during our second session in the short game that I will put an 8 iron in their hand near the end of the session. I will then ask each to proceed to hit a few half shots using the same concepts they are learning. This makes golf instruction a lot of fun as students hit shots that fly with dynamically improved compression. It is fun to see. After students ask to hit a few more and we do, we move right back to the short game development. This will encourage you also to learn these irrefutable concepts that will instinctively start infiltrating into your long game.

Once you have understood these principles and feel that for the most part you can accomplish the much needed feel, it is time to start into half-shot development.

However I would hope and even suggest that most of you reading this material would spend nearly six, 1.5-hour sessions before completely moving forward. If you would do that with your local well-trained PGA teaching professional that has experience teaching this way, then you would improve a staggering amount.

Next, continuing with your sand wedge and increase the backswing length to about hip high with the arms and the shaft in about a ninety-degree set angle.

Use your body to take the club back as you did in your chipping and pitching motion with everything moving together naturally as you have experienced in the short game process. The same holds true in the transition area as well continuing to use the bigger muscles of the arms, hips, and legs. You will still have the tendency to want to hit at the golf ball, but practice resisting these temptations, mastering the pressure points, and grip tension levels to break that old habit.

I personally like all students in these half swings to hit "the body-hold shot" at first similar to the pictures above. This is the same as the pitch, holding post-impact without completely releasing the clubhead, while keeping your arms in front of the turning body. Sort of a punch shot if you will with all angles, clubface, back of the left hand, and path intact connected to your turn. The finish side should be nearly the same length as the backswing side with the arms in front of your turn, the clubface toe up, and the left elbow now folding a bit as this finish side gets longer.

As extreme-holding practice I like to have these half shots held off, or as we say "bite off" even shorter on the finish side to have the student prove to me they can hold it without tension.

[The extreme bite-off finish of a pitch.]

That hold is so darn important, as players then become familiar with learning to control distances with the length of the swing, the clubface, and the body's movement rather than a hand thrash at the ball, which we know doesn't work at all. Many players have shared with us that previous distance controls were tough to gauge as the effective loft at impact was at times weaker than others. Many tell me that at times they are surprised that they were short since it felt like contact was fine. This inconsistent distance and face contact are absolutely related to inconsistent angular momentum and hold consistencies.

After a few practice sessions, students learn how to do this but yet create a powerful soft look to the holds, not having to squeeze the handle to death to get it to stop. The best players in the short-game area have developed great soft looking touch around the greens which translates to what appears to be an effortless full swing as well.

Now while we are here in the half shot, spend some time deciding how far your half swing sends the ball with your wedges. For the average male, the new loaded half swing with the 60-degree wedge is around 50-60 yards of carry. Find out yours with all your wedges at the same size with the same pace and rhythm throughout the entire motion. Do the same now with what you consider to be your two-thirds size of backswing and the corresponding two-thirds size of finish with the same exact tempo of all your wedges. Know these straight up yardages and have fun masterfully delivering them time and time again. With all new students, when we finally reach the end of the pitch type of shot instruction I will give many tests to prove their consistent angles. One particular test would be for the student to hit three half-size shots and tell me how far these shots will fly.

If you also can tell me the answer to that yardage and be consistently on it, then I am starting to believe you have got it in you to deliver it time and again. In other words you're starting to master the skill and slowly mastering the habit of that skill, so it is intuitive. Once consistency is achieved, we will then locate that exact distance from the flag on the pitching green, hitting several shots. Every shot should fall close to that exact money yardage. Happy times are arriving now with great excitement. Repeat the same with all your wedges in two-third-length shots. As a teacher I note here how the face angles, body movement, and the path are operating, providing hopefully more consistent delivery to impact.

Start also finding out what all your irons will deliver from these two-thirds backswing to two-thirds finish positions and exact tempos. You will then start to see that what appears to be a small swing is a very powerful golf swing. Take it a step further and allow the body and club to almost completely finish and note the differences between the hold type of finish and this abbreviated regular finish that has the same characteristics hopefully of the hold shots.

I have learned through experience it is at these times in this somewhat advanced stage of the short game development to now take a video of this two-third-size swing from all directions. Then take the time to sit down and compare this video side-by-side with the first full video workup on their first day of instruction that has never been reviewed.

The incredible adjustments made through our first few, short-game sessions have translated into their full motion, and they are ecstatic. This makes teaching so much fun.

[This is what I refer to as the 3/4body-connected finish that many of the great players employ. Master this shot, and you will hit consistent lasers.)

Take out your fairway wood and repeat the above practice. Then your driver, monitoring during your practice sessions all the short-game strategies that you worked so hard to accomplish. If you're smart you will move back and forth in your practice sessions from the short chips and pitches right into the 2/3 length of swings and you will start to see and hear things that you never thought possible.

It is so fun to hit golf shots like that.

REAL-TIME SKILL
AND MIND PRACTICE

A few words about what we term as "real-time practice." Real-time practice is preparation practice that mirrors the way the game is played. I believe students should divide half of their practice sessions into "preparation" to play the game. After all, why do we practice? Is it not so we can play and enjoy the game much more by hitting better shots, pitches, and putts when we play or in various competitions?

So in our case here, once you have spent several, good-quality weeks relearning the long game through the short-game techniques substantially acquiring a good percentage of these skills, split up your practice sessions. Divide each practice into working on your new-skills development then the other half into one-ball practice. An example would be if you had a nice one and a half-hour block of practice time in the short-game pitch and chips practice, spend the first forty-five minutes with the new-skills training then the other forty-five minutes with one of your own personal balls, pitching it to your intended target. Retrieve that ball and toss it to a new area, repeating this from various distances all around the green. All this is done without mechanical thought even if you miss a few shots. Start practicing trusting that you have created some decent *habits* already. It is mentally important to practice developing this trust practice so you get comfortable with your new habits. A fun little game that nearly all our players' play starts with choosing three-hole locations on the chipping green. Play one ball each to these flags from the same location using your choice of chip and pitch clubs. If one of the balls is not within a certain preset chosen distance, then you must start over at that location. Once you achieve all three then move on to the second location, and so on. You can even complete this drill by putting out if your practice greens are decent. We have as many as six locations all with different type lies for all three shots. Do all this with the *intent* to practice forgetting about what you have been working on, totally focusing on how you see the shot visually, possibly where you would like it to land, and imagining how it rolls out all instinctively one shot at a time. Do not improve the lie the ball settles into but play it real time as if you're on the course with many of your locations being different lies and uneven hills. The same holds true for your long-game practice and you're putting as well. This type of practice will start to prepare you for the course and your brain will recognize you as a well-prepared, trustworthy, one-shot practice player.

Once you seem to have acquired your new short game skills, do not discontinue practicing these shots. Again my opinion is that every warm-up session prior to your play and also every practice session should always start out with your short-game work revisited. Every time! I would include fifteen minutes of your pre-round warm-ups in these little, short-game fundamentals on the range before ever advancing to the full swing. Then warm into your full swings without a single mechanical thought. You desire these fundamentals to be so ingrained that they become subconscious habit. It is then that they will start to be instinctively engrained in pressure competitions. All students eventually are able to create their own personalized, abbreviated, short-shot, warm-up routines for daily practice that accelerate growth. Everyone is unique, of course; therefore, each player's abbreviated programs cover their own individual needs for feel, training, and skill acquisition. Eventually you will be able to pick and choose what is pertinent that seems to accelerate your development.

Real-Time Mental Practice

Right from your beginning development it is well-advised to initiate development of the mental techniques that are associated with each area of the game. Everyone needs to understand how to manage their emotions and thoughts on the golf course, which in my opinion is the definition of the "mental game." Accordingly we share step-by-step prudent mental techniques with all students as they progress in their physical and mental development.

Obviously there are several new important areas of necessary physical technique to learn and progress toward as is the purpose of this book. However, they all need to be coupled with a "brain fitness program" if you will, added to each practice session.

Realizing that most noncompetitive golfers have little time during the week to practice and play, there has to be in place a realistic acceleration "road-mapped" plan to improve. Dividing your practice into working on this new physical training, along with brain training, real-time practice plays an important role in development.

Creating a physical and mental fitness pre-shot routine formula that translates on the golf course and in competition is what everyone is after. Every player has to learn the tools that assist them internally to create that easy soft sort of play that seems to be the ingredient for all good rounds. This book is not primarily a mental instructional or peak performance type of book but with that said, all skill learning has to be accompanied by mental translation to some extent. Just learning *only* technique will not work as you take that over-trained mechanical brain to the course and find that it is not enough. That is precisely why each practice needs to be divided into developing the technical information and into real-time belief and trusting applications. I think it is fair to say that *trusting your ability to execute the shot is the bottom line of the entire mental game.* Free from all the worry, doubts, and uncertainties that we "choose" and allow to be present in our minds. For sure it is a choice that we have but darn hard to overcome, especially if you do not have the proper skills to start with which at least gives one a better-than-average chance of hitting decent shots. This is why we diligently practice our skill, so that these skills can become habit and instinctive to us. Once they become a habit we can then transfer these habits to our subconscious mind where confidence *lives*. If our habits end up at *that* location, then under all pressure circumstances we will always revert to those habits. Then let the fun begin!

Couple these with a smart-brain-type fitness program that exercises ones mental information processes and you have players that can let shots go with no attachments, full of self-efficacy. The wonderful truth about creating this ideal performance state is it is nowhere near as elusive as players think. It can be the most beautiful part of the game available to every player.

There is a simple drill that I would like each of you to try in your next practice session. After initiating your new short-game instruction practice take a couple minutes and hit five chips to a given target on the green. After those five shots are completed, hit another five shots to no target but just to a random location with absolutely no care about the result. Note the differences in the results and the different feelings with the random shots versus the target shots. What would be the reason the random no-target shots are almost always so much better in contact, consistency, and ease? Simply these random shots had no expectations associated, had no baggage of penalty associated, and had an anxiety-free delivery to them. There was a huge element of unrecognized trust associated with all five of those shots. Trust is a big part of developing your personalized ideal internal state that has huge ramifications in developing your game.

In our programs we share the three T's. They represent *tension*, *tempo*, and *trust*. We have found that developing these three key words and their corresponding internal meanings has significant, accelerated influence in early development. These words seem to advance major freedom from the fear of outcome that seems to paralyze many players.

THE THREE Ts

Tension

In your practice sessions, learn what too much tension is as you body-scan each area of your anatomy from the neck down. Find out what a good tension percentage should be that seems to create more consistent shots in your short-game development. Just saying the word *relax* most of the time does not translate well, but creating inside your pre-shot routine a feeling of tension release achieved and developed in practice is! Learn not only what your tension level is that seems to work well but also learn how to monitor that level during the short shot development. Practice often holding your finish and ask the self-scanning question of your tension number throughout your swing. Find out the tension percentage number that seems to be the right choice for your best consistent contact and practice this in each session. You will be simply amazed at the outcomes.

Tempo

When you have developed your own short-game tempo and rhythm flow that we spoke of earlier in this book and made this your own through diligent practice, you have found something that most never find. If you cultivate rhythmic tempo in your real-time practice, adding this to your pre-shot physical and mental routines and can under the gun deliver that tempo, you will be astounded how well you play. This physical tempo is also a mental tempo in your walk, your brain, your eyes, your routine, and every area of life for that matter. Add this type of training to your practice sessions and include it right into your on-course play and competitions. By the way, it can easily be added right to the tension level as well, making both of these *family relatives*. Make them part of your routine on each shot.

Trust

Learning to trust what you have worked so hard to train is a big mental component that separates the average players from the great players. *Trusting* attaches no expectations of the outcome of any shot, and this frees students to be instinctive players that play in-the-moment golf with no additional baggage of previous or future outcomes. The wonderful thing about these three simple Ts is that we all can develop and train them right into our games right alongside the development of the technical skills. The mind and the body must run the race together and developing one without the other is a big mistake. That is why you train the mind with real-time practice complete with your entire on course pre-shot and thought routines. You will soon find that your best play will likely be totally *without* how-to's attached in any way. Soon the three Ts will become *one* T and all without thought of any kind. All instinctive and fun. A lot of my students write a large *T* on their golf gloves that just reminds them of their thoughts for the day. Others even draw a *T* on their golf ball that not only reminds them, but also serves alignment purposes for putting and tee shots. For our students around the world we create a "mind card" that all use in practice and eventually create their personalized ideal internal formula for each shot. This card is kept in the pocket and referred to until it is locked in the subconscious. Once there, then each student has their own mental management formula for competitive play.

On the front side of the card we remind players of the reason for practice, and on the other side a possible order that promotes instinctive play without attachments.

You Practice for:

1. SKILL DEVELOPMENT
2. TRANSFER TO SUBCONSCIOUS
3. HABIT MAKING FOR PRESSURE
4. TRUST DEVELOPMENT
5. AUTOMATIC + INSTINCTIVE

The back side of the card takes each student on a step-by-step, simple, orderly mental progression to create automatic and instinctive. It can include the following:

1. RELAXATION
2. BREATHING
3. HEART BEAT
4. MATCH (BODY/MIND)
5. PRE-SHOT PLAN - TIMES
6. VISUALS - CONCENTRATION
7. PLAYER 1 - PLAYER 2
8. COMMITMENT - FOCUS
9. TENSION, TEMPO, TRUST

These words should all have personal meaning to players, and should all be personalized to fit your mental performance acceleration.

A FEW FINAL WORDS
ABOUT SWING PLANE

People chase around their swing plane their entire life on the practice tee. They know they tend to come over the top and create an outside-in approach, causing severe spin at times on the golf ball, resulting in slices and pull hooks. However everyone can learn intelligent path through short-game feel instruction. Continuing in that vain, I also *don't* believe it is natural for the human being to swing on the needed angled incline plane at a *golf ball that is motionless on the ground*. If it were, we would be helping many more people learn how to get more outside. Since it is somewhat unnatural for us to swing back on an inclined plane and even doubly hard for us to achieve that same incline on the forward swing, we had better once again spend just a little more time here.

For discussion purposes let's say at address the inclined shaft plane line is approximately fifty degrees. This is the shaft plane we would love to return to at impact, but there are many forces fighting us for that plane which want to send us in a different direction.

With wedge in hand again making half swings, we know it is a lot easier to learn this plane then it is if we just slug it out with long shots. Learning the correct plane loading feel into the forefinger pads, the left and right wrists plane lines, and thumbs is paramount.

Coming up with drills that accelerate this feel as mentioned earlier goes a long way toward swing plane-accelerated development.

The simple act of placing a long tee in the grip end or using an additional attached shaft that can be used to point at the target line will go a long way toward your growth in accelerated-plane development. The study of this is the feel that the correct load creates so you can create it at will.

[Adding the extra shaft for plane feel and visual development accelerates learning.]

Once you have felt that on-plane feel and corresponding locations of the feel well enough, you will be able to master it. Practice these half to two-third-size swings a lot, hitting shots without much effort focusing on the backswing plane feel and pressure point loads first.

Once you have attained this portion, refocus your thought back to the forward swing plane. With good lower-body posture, create what we refer to as "pump drills." From a partial near two-thirds backswing length start moving forward into the downswing and stop while still on plane. Check your plane and the corresponding feel of the pressure points on the correct plane. You should be able to see the butt end of your shaft pointing at the ball or the target line. Pump this back and forth memorizing that forward swing plane feeling that seems to be quiet elusive to millions of golfers.

Back and forth, continue the pump drill, matching the loads and the lower body, moving in all synchronized detail right on plane. Try this first with small half-size swings and then graduate into bigger swings. Try this with your eyes closed as well with surrounding mirrors and then check your positions. Once you feel you can master the arm delivery and plane moves proceed to hit several two-thirds size 8 irons. Take inventory of the certain feels you have learned in this book that are paramount to a great solid ball flight. You will start to note many different feelings, such as your shoulders, and how they seem to hold as you initiate your forward swings. All this accomplished without verbal commands to do so. If you have the opportunity, it is prudent to weekly video your swings and movements to see how close you are coming to your strength holds and planes. Then going over and over the feel and visual learning necessary for you to finally capture the movements in full. Your ball flight and impact of course are true indicators, but these little quick videos will go a long way to assist that. The new pocket-size cameras on the market today that can take a short video are awesome little tools that many of our instructors use for immediate, quick feedback in sessions. So if you have the means to take a video once in a while, I highly support that.

"GOLF'S FIELD"

Field Club Programming
Understanding The Body's Harmony Field

Science continues to find that this awesome supernatural body of ours continues to be the most amazing machine. Year after year and decade after decade, new anatomy discoveries are made, and likely, it will never stop. This also was proven to be true as scientists began to deeply understand our "electric bodies" and initiated research of our body's "electrical magnetic fields." In the early 1940s, discoveries were made in the medical community of ways to measure the separate magnetic fields of all organs of the body, including all levels of the brain. This nonintrusive means of taking a good look inside each organ's field was a big deal then and has enormous ramifications today for me as a golf professional, instructor, and coach. I was privileged to meet Takashi Ohara, a sports and life enhancement specialist in the early 1990s, during one of my many trips instructing in Japan and Korea. His work in the study of the human anatomy and functions of the brain were very intriguing to me. Takashi was the first to consider that we can possibly use the body's electrical field to measure and enhance mental performance in competition and in life for that matter. I initially researched his findings by purchasing several books about our body's magnetic field and discovered what he said had merit and quite possibly we could use it for our student's mental development. From our first introduction we embarked on a long wonderful journey to this present day of developing a way to measure all body functions and brain chemistry that relates to sports performance. With these fantastic measurements and the equipment to do so, we can now use the information to springboard our students to heights never before imagined not only in golf, but in life as well. Now for well over a decade we have created a quantified way to measure some of the mental areas of golf performance and thought. Armed with this information we then have data to help players adjust and improve these measurements.

"The Harmony Field"

The ability to read the electromagnetic fields of the human body, mind, and emotions using LFT machines has become a magnificent way to locate areas of significance regarding athletic performance.

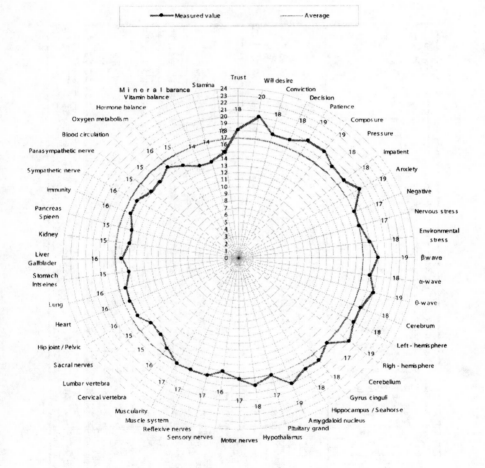

[This graph is the typical illustration of the many parts
of the body and brain we measure.]

We have now tested well over 2,000 professional golfers, Olympic champions, political figures, junior champions, and everyday people. The results of this testing gives feedback to our instructors that can be measured and calculated for students to clearly see. The differences of these measurements in the golf sector of tour professionals and those wishing to be are quite significant. Armed with this information and a plan for adjustment, we can clearly present to students a clear, well-marked physical and mental road map of improvement. These improvements consistently improve performance.

1	Trust	19	19	18	19	19	18	19	19	19	18.78
2	Will desire	18	19	19	19	19	20	18	18	18	18.67
3	Conviction	19	18	20	20	20	18	18	18	19	18.89
4	Decision	20	18	19	18	19	18	20	18	19	18.78
5	Patience	18	19	18	18	18	19	18	20	18	18.44
6	Composure	18	18	19	19	18	19	19	(17)	18	18.33
7	Pressure	18	18	18	18	18	18	18	18	18	18.00
8	Impatient	17	19	17	17	19	18	18	17	17	17.67
9	Anxiety	18	18	17	18	18	19	17	18	18	17.89
10	Negative	18	20	18	18	18	17	18	19	17	18.11
11	Nervous stress	17	19	17	17	19	17	18	18	17	17.67
12	Environmental stress	18	17	18	17	18	18	17	18	18	17.67
13	β-wave	18	18	18	18	19	19	17	17	17	17.89
14	α-wave	19	19	18	19	18	18	19	19	18	18.56
15	θ-wave	18	19	19	18	20	19	19	18	19	18.78
16	Cerebrum	17	19	18	18	18	18	18	18	17	17.89
17	Left - hemisphere	18	18	19	18	19	18	18	18	18	18.22
18	Righ - hemisphere	18	19	18	19	19	19	19	17	17	18.33
19	Cerebellum	18	18	18	17	17	17	18	18	18	17.67
20	Gyrus cinguli	17	18	17	16	18	18	18	17	17	17.33
21	Hippocampus / Seahorse	17	17	18	17	17	18	18	17	16	17.22
22	Amygdaloid nucleus	17	17	17	17	17	19	17	16	17	17.11
23	Pituitary grand	16	18	17	16	18	17	18	17	16	17.00
24	Hypothalamus	16	17	18	17	17	18	19	16	16	17.11
25	Motor nerves	17	16	16	16	16	17	16	16	16	16.22
26	Sensory nerves	16	17	16	16	16	16	16	17	17	16.33
27	Reflexive nerve	16	16	17	17	17	17	15	16	15	16.22
28	Muscle system	15	16	16	15	16	17	16	15	16	15.78
29	Muscularity	16	17	16	15	17	17	16	15	15	16.00
30	Cervical vertebra	16	15	16	14	15	16	14	14	15	15.00
31	Lumbar vertebra	14	14	15	14	15	15	14	14	14	14.33
32	Sacral nerves	15	14	15	(13)	14	15	15	15	14	14.44
33	Pelvic	14	14	14	(13)	14	16	14	14	15	14.22
34	Heart	14	16	14	14	15	16	16	16	15	15.11
35	Lung	14	15	15	16	16	16	16	16	16	15.56
36	Stomach / Intseines	16	14	15	16	14	15	16	15	15	15.11
37	Liver / Gallblader	15	15	15	15	14	16	15	16	15	15.11
38	Kidney	14	14	14	14	15	15	14	16	15	14.56
39	Pancreas / Spleen	15	15	14	14	14	15	15	14	14	14.44
40	Immunity	15	14	15	15	16	16	15	16	14	15.11
41	Sympathetic nerve	15	15	16	14	15	16	16	16	15	15.33
42	Parasympathetic nerve	14	14	15	15	16	15	15	15	14	14.78
43	Blood circulation	14	14	15	15	14	15	15	15	14	14.56
44	Oxygen metabolism	14	15	14	14	14	16	16	16	15	14.89
45	Hormone balance	15	15	13	13	15	15	14	14	14	14.22
46	Vitamin balance	14	14	13	14	14	14	13	13	13	(13.55)
47	Mineral barance	13	13	14	13	14	14	14	13	13	(13.44)
48	Stamina	15	15	16	15	15	15	15	14	16	15.11
01~48	Average	16.31	16.58	16.50	16.21	16.69	16.92	16.60	16.40	16.19	16.49
01~06	mind	18.67	18.50	18.83	18.83	18.83	18.67	18.67	18.33	18.50	18.65
07~12	stress	17.67	18.50	17.50	17.50	18.33	17.83	17.67	18.00	17.50	17.83
13~18	brain	18.00	18.67	18.33	18.33	18.83	18.50	18.33	17.83	17.67	18.28
19~27	potential	16.67	17.11	17.11	16.56	17.00	17.44	17.22	16.67	16.44	16.91
28~33	athlete	15.00	15.00	15.33	14.00	15.17	16.00	14.83	14.50	14.83	14.96
34~39	body	14.67	14.83	14.50	14.83	14.67	15.50	15.33	15.50	15.00	14.98
40~44	immunity	14.40	14.40	15.00	14.60	15.00	15.60	15.40	15.60	14.40	14.93
45~48	nutrition	14.25	14.25	14.00	13.75	14.50	14.50	14.00	13.50	14.00	14.08
01~27	mind barance	17.63	18.07	17.85	17.67	18.11	18.04	17.89	17.59	17.41	17.81
28~48	body barance	14.62	14.67	14.76	14.33	14.86	15.48	14.95	14.86	14.62	14.79
	difference	3.01	3.41	3.09	3.33	3.25	2.56	2.94	2.74	2.79	3.01

[This graph indicates a couple of physical areas of immediate concern that I circled. Many additional low scoring areas had to also be addressed and students given a quantified way to work toward better numbers.]

Our program goal is simple: To create a good understanding of not only what is harmony in golf and life, but much more understand and incorporate meaningful accelerated mental foundational principles that create this harmony for improved golf performance. Creating what I have termed "harmony balance" is what all players are really after. Saving you the need to listen to any more boring details and need to study electromagnetic fields, I wanted to for the first time introduce to you just a couple of the many techniques that may give you a better understanding of "golf harmony."

For the last twenty years or so, there has been zealous study in the mental area of sports. Through these studies we have come to recognize that being "in the flow" or in what has been referred to as the "zone" enhances performance. Most would say it is pretty darn elusive to catch even a glimpse of this flow state.

Before we close the final chapters of this book, I wanted to present to you a few, long researched harmony flow tempo exercises you can use in your game (Short game first, please.). These have been proven time and again to create personal harmony and the aforementioned machine numbers prove it for *every* student.

1. Field tempo is not just about short-game and long-game physical tempo but more importantly, one's walking tempo, thinking tempo, breathing tempo, and even-eye movement tempo. This is precisely why we set up the walking tempo referred to earlier in the book so we can share the important mental values of your pace. So for drill, create your pacing tempo and learn to walk that tempo during your competitive golf rounds. Practice rethinking it especially after poor shots and miscues where each step fulfils a clear picture of calmness, commitment, and trust. Once you have established what your best walking-tempo performance state is, use this same tempo in your everyday life. Oftentimes we find in stressful life situations we all have the unfortunate ability to mentally ping-pong all the possible negative thoughts that could happen. The *what ifs*, I call them, and they move at constant rates of rapid acceleration. This ping-pong effect even in our lives really hampers mental and harmony performance. The way you move about and the pace in your life will be a direct reflection of how you perform as well.

Learning to pace your thoughts, creating positive images, dealing rationally with possible outcomes in tempo is what you are after. Even your music, movements outside of golf, genuine smile, the tempo in which you move your eyes, and a host of other activities will promise to assist your golf development.

2. Practice swing tempo and tension. Earlier you learned a valuable way of using the metronome to discover your short-game easy flow. Couple this with a tension number and we have created an element of soft calmness and trust with each shot. This is a huge accelerated-performance technique that will immediately transition into much better play. It is important for all players, regardless of skill level, to discover not only where their tension is, but also how to self-regulate it with ease. These tension levels are located in your arms, hands, shoulders, neck, legs, stomach, and back. Our research shows that relaxing the back of the head, neck, and shoulders seems to be a major physical key to relaxing the other areas in a sort of chain reaction.

However each player needs to find out themselves by experimentation which area seems to be the key for unlocking trust and clarity in competitive golf. Start with the back of the head and neck area however, and allow the release of all the stored-up tension in this area take the pressure off all the rest of the areas of the body. Experiment with all these tension areas and find the one for you that seems to be the ultimate key to releasing all tension areas. Add this as the trigger in which you initiate your pre-shot routine and you have already surpassed most players around the world. Learn them using these short shots first, as it is real tough to learn it immediately in the long game. Once you feel you can pinch contact any type of short shot with these tension releases, then you're well on your way, believe me. For drill hit shots with 80 percent tension, then 70 percent, 60 percent, 50 percent, and so on, until you find your personal comfort number. In our programs we have developed for each student their go-to mental numbers.

An example that several of our tournament players have incorporated in the pre-shot routine are the numbers 70—40. This translates to 70 percent effort coupled with 40 percent tension.

It also sets up immediately a quantified mental picture of *trust*. That word and its corresponding accelerated-performance value is everything, for if you can discover how to trust, you will become a significant player.

3. Another tempo in this harmony field is tempo of eye movement. Since the eyes are the light of the heart and the heart reflects the person, it is imperative to learn how to use them. Moving your eyes and even your neck and head inside your personalized tempo field creates great harmony in the heart and your heart feeds the brain with valuable information which is reflected in your face. You can observe players quick-snap turns of the head, eyes, and neck in their routines on regular chips and shots and dramatically in their putts as well. You know when you see this there is something amiss internally. So your practice in all areas of the game using the discoveries included in this book can eventually include matching your walk, body, thought, mind, eyes, and heart. For each of you, start out developing how to move your eyes in a rhythm sequence that seems to match your regular rhythm walk. Practice turning even your head in that same rhythm when you putt, or hit all shots. That pace will surely translate right into your mental game by sending great signals to your heart and brain that everything is well under control and that you trust the outcome of each shot. These little field tempo ideas will go a long way toward introducing you to better mental clarity and golf chemistry.

A FEW WORDS
ABOUT HEARTMATH

Players learn quickly, mostly after the fact, that negative mental scrambling on the golf course can happen so fast. This translates into many students being only one shot away from big problems in a round. I find that it's almost like players are waiting for the negative shot, even on the edge of their seat in anticipation of the wheels falling off, regardless of how well they are playing. Even to the point that many say after hitting a good shot "they had a sense of great relief." That is so telling and sad to me as a mental game instructor. It sure does not have to be this way for anyone. It's normal to have some negative emotions or anxiety on occasion; yet the greatest discovery is how to shift out of negative attitudes fast—yes, even immediately in the middle of your round. The power to quickly shift attitude and emotion is available to every player, regardless of their current golf level. So many players allow typical fear, worry, anxiety, frustration, anger, and blame to drain the very energy they need for confidence and better performance. Negative feelings and attitudes can run like an undercurrent and drain your energy even while you're "trying to think positive," trying to visualize a great shot or repeat an affirmation. Then you wonder why the mental game techniques you have tried aren't working for you. It's because your internal feelings affect your shots and feeling has a direct correlation to ease of play or, as I call it, "instinctive golf" or "IT." To improve your mental performance as well as your game and your well-being, it's imperative to take control of your emotions. Here is a fourth possibility of the twelve that we use in our "Harmony Programs."

You can become concretely more aware of what your emotions are doing in the moment and how they affect your game. HeartMath techniques show how you can take control of your emotions, enabling you to make dramatic improvements in your game and more importantly, in your life. You'll come to understand that it is the emotions behind the tension, negative inner dialogue, or a distracting thought that creates self-judgment, lack of confidence, and an almost paralyzing fear for many.

Research shows the following consequences of negative emotions:

- Reduced physical coordination
- Less ability to think clearly
- Less efficiency in decision making
- Higher risk of high blood pressure

Research shows the following consequences of positive emotions:

- Improved coordination
- Faster reaction times
- More flexibility in the way you think
- Improved hormonal balance and longer life span

In the energetic aspects of golf, emotions are the key. The missing performance factor for many golfers is the ability to regain your emotional equilibrium and recover mental and physical energy when you're halfway through a round and struggling. Once insecurity and self-doubt creep in, erosion of your normal physical golf attributes starts to show up. Those strong emotions cause a huge drop in energy and confidence as well as focus and coordination. This is because emotions are linked to physiology in the human bioelectrical system. These emotions and swings in hormonal balance show up immediately in our field-program readings. Insecurity and self-doubt can immediately skew your motor skills. This is primarily why we include these techniques in our programs. They have been proven to assist students to self-adjust their stress levels at will. The fact is that golf skill training and mental training are not enough by themselves. *You have to address the emotions directly.* Otherwise a lack of emotional equilibrium can affect your balance, timing, and swing rhythm.

Over the thirty-seven years that I have been a golf teacher and coach, I have been a relentless pursuer of tools for healthy mental and emotional balance. Over and over I've found once the physical foundation is set and becomes habit, it's the single most important component for successful performances. Yet it's also one of the most difficult areas to teach. Most players only catch a glimpse of what "mental control" as many kids call it feels like. This despite all the catch phrases and tons of literature they may have studied over the years. Mental control methods are missing a most important element of how-to process.

When I was first introduced to the Institute of HeartMath, I was immediately impressed with the amount of science and research that had gone into their techniques. When I find any promising tool, mind process, or technique, I first test it on myself, staff, and a few hand-picked students. I needed proof that HeartMath was not just another set of mental techniques that would fail during the heat of battle. I found these techniques surprisingly effective and simple in my first tests, but in order to effectively compare data I put several students on our launch monitor equipment and took baseline averages of ball flight, swing speed, and path lines. I then explained the science behind HeartMath and how HeartMath's Quick Coherence technique changes their heart rate variability pattern and emotional perception to improve performance. Practicing the technique for one minute effectively shifts emotions and achieves heart and emotional synchronicity, which students were able to monitor and receive instant feedback using the Em Wave PC Stress Relief System Software. The technique is simple enough that most students managed some level of synchronization the first time as measured by the Em Wave PC software. This was an important step in understanding their heart's role in emotional control.

[Working with HeartMath software.]

Returning to the launch monitor after their HeartMath practice, the results were so staggering, I was shocked. For every single student, clubhead speed increased and ball fight improved. For 75 percent of the students, every measure improved.

We then tested the Em Wave PC software outdoors hitting real-time golf shots. Again distance and ball flight control improved with remarkable consistency. Even though the students I tested, from top-level professionals, collegians, to amateurs, were astounded by their improvements, it was not until I used the HeartMath software with my family and friends and saw the emotional benefits outside of golf did it sink in for me that something incredible was happening.

Next, while teaching in Japan, I was asked by HeartMath staff to test more than sixty-five of the Japanese golf teachers that I instruct along with several tour professionals all practicing Quick Coherence with the Em Wave PC. I personally wanted to see how the electromagnetic field test numbers would compare to the old numbers each teacher had established. In every area that we quantify for golfers, every professional's electromagnetic readings revealed dramatic improvements. My colleagues in Japan that I work with in our field programs were surprised to see readings in some cases comparable to those of Japan's Olympic champions. You can imagine the buzz these sessions caused.

I now have a better understanding of how powerful this research is, why it works, and how it can improve the game of golf and also people's lives. As a result, I am a much more effective teacher, simply because we now have an additional important quantified tool that can assist players with the ability to actually control the way they feel and think. Even the most timid and fearful golfers can become emotionally synchronized and able to achieve goals they never thought possible. Many of our players use the Em Wave PC. Their golf is improving as is their confidence and joy in the game. The results simply cannot be disputed.

So I add this little information in our field area for you to digest and play a bit with. Take a look at http://www.heartmath.com/ and catch a little more information about the beautiful science of HeartMath.

Note: The following information in this book reflects the authors experience and research and is not intended to replace individual medical advice. Before beginning these exercises consult your physician or other appropriate health professionals.

MORNING GOLF-SPECIFIC WORKOUT

The morning workout described here is *only* for the purpose of promoting proper pelvic hold movements, better complete posture including upper and lower back, much needed strength building in appropriate wrist movements, and enough flexibility in these areas to create impact. I suppose many reading this material will pass this over but it is a mistake. If I could give you a pill to create proper hip delivery, correct action with your hands, pressure point path, and a safe back, many would take it. Well, your pill is about 10-15 minutes in the morning each day that will promote everything you have read. Now this is not your daily workout, cardio, or weight training, but it *will* promote your golf improvement. I want to thank Dr. Paul for helping me years ago learn the value of simple Golf-specific static and ballistic exercises and stretches that influence health and performance.

1. My opinion based on what I have learned through the years is that all golfers need to be flat on their back with legs on a stool or a ball at a ninety-degree angle every day of their life. This gravity exercise promotes flattening the entire back, removes any roundness of the upper regions in the golf setup, and also promotes lower back health. Hold and flatten for several minutes and even longer on the mornings when you have the time.

1A. Adding to this simple gravity back exercise is what Dr. Callaway calls

STATIC BACK ACCUPRESSURE

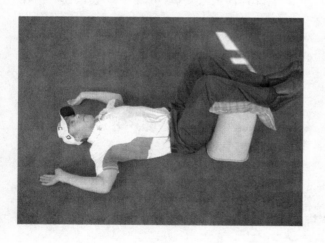 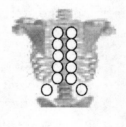

Instructions

- Lie on your back on a firm surface (padded carpeting) with your hips and knees supported on a couch, bed, ball, or chair in the 90°/90° position.
- Position two golf balls or tougher two tennis balls on each side of your lower spine—in the soft tissue spaces that are located

several inches lateral from your spine, above your pelvic bones and below your ribs (Note: You will know when you have the balls properly positioned when you are resting down on the balls and you feel a mildly uncomfortable pressure in the muscles of your lower back.). If the tennis balls are too tough to start with, then try two golf balls at first and then eventually graduate to the tennis balls.

- Slowly reach your arms up and out into the 90°/90° position.
- Support your head, shoulders, and arms as needed with pillows or a stack of towels as needed.
- *Hold* this gentle acupressure position until you feel a *complete* melting/softening of the initial pressure from the balls in your lower back. This is an awesome exercise for the cupped lower back, the rounded midback problems, and also the pelvic collapse that I speak of so much in this book. I also ask students to locate and push their fingers into the (ASIS) hip joints to feel and promote the proper pelvic movements in the game.
- Repeat each day. About three minutes or more.

Purpose

- Releases tightness in the lower back muscles, reduces rounded upper back, forward-tipped shoulders, and forward head.
- Improves your ability to perform the pelvic tilt that I want from each player and assists the ideal 'power' positions throughout the full swing.

2. THE KNEE HUGGER'S STRETCH (two minutes)

Remove the tennis balls and transition right from the acupressure position to the knee hugger's position. With your entire back touching the floor in every area possible from the neck down, exhale slowly as you curl your knees toward your chest as close possible. Hug your knees and *gently pull* them a bit closer without giving up your flat back position. Concentrate on contracting your lower abdomen driving it into the floor. Keep the upper back and shoulders dead weight flat on the floor as you pull your knees toward you. Exhale and repeat for at least four breaths total. After a while you should be able to do the advanced exercise with your hands at your side and pressed firmly into the ground, curling your knees to your chest without assistance. This stretch is an additional lower back and mid back assistant for the lower body's training that is paramount to becoming consistent.

Next, do the hugger one leg at a time with the other leg flat on the floor. Follow the same procedure as above.

[This age old stretch and strengthener has been around since I have been playing golf. It never grows old and is the grandfather of back stretches. I recommend it for students every single day without fail.]

3. Next straight from this position stretch the hamstrings, one leg at a time while on your back, extending one leg up using your hands to lightly hold and pull a tiny bit at a time or against a wall with the other leg flat on the floor. Gradually stretch your heel, making your foot flat for additional stretch. Start this slow and not a full ninety-degree extension in the beginning but a bit more week by week until it is quite easy. Eventually this hamstring stretch will go a long way, promoting many of the important hip and back areas we have spoken about throughout this book. Each leg at least four breaths.

[Gently hold the thigh and take your time gradually improving each week]

(Picture A)   (Picture B)

Instructions for the wall hamstring stretch

- Lie on your back with one leg straight up against the edge of a wall/open door and your other leg bent (Picture A).
- Adjust your body position either closer or farther from the wall, as needed, so that you feel a comfortable stretch behind your stretch leg positioned up against the wall.

- When you feel as though you have the proper body distance from the wall and comfortable degree of stretch behind your stretch leg, slide your other leg flat to the floor (Picture B).
- Then to begin the stretch, gently straighten the knee *and* bend the ankle of your stretch leg down toward you—this will enhance the stretch feeling!
- *Hold* this gentle stretch position until you feel a *complete* melting/softening of the initial stretch.
- As the stretch feeling gradually releases, you may want to slide closer to the wall.
- Repeat both sides.

Purpose

- * To assist each player naturally with the ability to retain the pelvic joints.
- Releases tightness in the back of the hips and legs, making it a ton easier to move into solid impact posts.
- Improves posture at address and restores proper bending function.
- Reduces strain and injury potential in your spine, hips, and legs during the complete golf swing.

4. Crossover leg and hip rotation stretch and strengthening exercise.

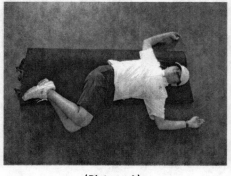

(Picture A)   (Picture B)

Instructions

- Lie on your back with both legs bent and feet flat on the floor.
- Reach one arm up and out into the 'tray' (90°/90°) position (Note: If this position creates uncomfortable strain on your shoulder, simply rest your arm at your side with your palm facing up.).
- Slowly rotate your knees away from your stabilized shoulder until you feel a gentle stretch in your spine, chest, and shoulder, and/or hip regions. You may gently apply downward pressure on your rotated knees with your opposite hand to assist the stretch, but start slow and eventually get there
- *Hold* this gentle stretch position until you feel a melting/softening of the initial gentle stretch in your spine, chest and shoulder, and/or hip regions.
- Place your fingers in the hip area shared with earlier in this book to feel the necessary pelvic hold we speak about. Doing this will go a long way toward your recognition of how it should feel.
- Switch to the other side.

Purpose

- Releases tightness in the spine, chest, shoulder, outer hip and thigh regions.
- Improves your ability to rotate your spine while still maintaining the most important hip areas throughout the short game and full swing.
- Reduces stress and injury potential to your lower back, shoulders, hips, knees, and ankles.

5. Lie on your back once again with both legs folded in a near ninety-degree angle suspended in the air. Put your fingers in the hip sockets that we shared earlier in your short-game development and place a light ball or balloon between your knees. Next slightly a little at a time allow your legs some rotations to the left and then the right while applying some pressure by pushing down on the hip socket areas. This awesome stretch will go a long way toward

you developing the correct pelvic tilt in the golf swing. Hold each side for at least four breaths and then repeat once again. This is an exercise you need to do the balance of your golfing life.

6. Next cross each leg completely over the other until your leg touches the ground. Do your best to keep your shoulders flat on the ground as you work that stretch. Start simple and work your way to being able to completely lay that leg over. This great daily exercise has been around for ions and it promotes so many needed things in our game such as turn, hip holds, lower-back stretch, and many safety issues. Hold for one minute, continuing to push your hand in each hip area. Switch sides.

7. To promote stretch and most importantly strengthen the wrist areas that play such a huge role in power, path delivery, consistent pure contact, and target trajectory development.

STRENGTHENING THE WRIST ANGLES

Picture A   Picture B

Picture C   Picture D

Instructions:

- Start with the right hand at your side with the normal left hand grip.

- Slowly, elevate the clubhead out in front of you just holding for four breaths keeping that back of the left wrist flat (Picture A). For some, this will feel quite heavy at first so choke well down on the club until it feels a bit more comfortable
- Next create a ninety-degree shaft to left arm position keeping the left wrist flat. The left elbow may bend slightly but keep it as soft straight as possible (Fig. B). Hold for four breaths.
- Bring that club back to airborne impact complete with a flat strong looking left wrist that may even have a bowed look promoting impact (Fig. C).
- Finally promote post impact by rotating your completely flat left wrist position (Fig. D).
- Next put both hands on the club and assume your address posture and start memorizing that wrist set on plane in the backswing. Hold that feeling for at least one breath and then return those set angles slowly to impact feeling the proper pressure points discussed earlier. Repeat as often as you have the time. I think you all know how important that is as you teach your brain this new memory wrist on plane deep delivery positioning.

Purpose

- First and foremost it teaches you the proper wrist sets in both hands eliminating all kinds of possible errors.
- Improves the strength of your wrists and forearms that play such a vital role. This is why the old timers used to carry that little weighted club around all the time setting and delivering the wrists angles. It served them well. The wonderful thing about this simple forgotten exercise is that it *transfers*.
- Improves your feel of correct plane, clubface, and delivery angles.
- Promotes your ability to create natural angular momentum all on correct path.
- Provides a ton of injury protection to all kinds of golf related common injury areas. I like the fact that this exercise also removes some of the possibility of related elbow tendonitis.

WRISTS TURNS

(Easier beginning drill holding the shaft in the middle)

(A bit more difficult with the left hand on the end of the grip)

Instructions

- Sit or stand and correctly hold a s/w in your left hand with your elbow softly straight.
- Slowly, rotate your hand, wrist, and forearm until the clubhead has rotated as far as possible to the opposite direction never allowing any wrist cup or flexation. Hold these positions briefly as you move back and forth.

- Repeat often during the day, being careful however to not over do this in the beginning but gradually work toward the necessary strength desired for pure impact and post impact.
- Repeat this drill in your right hand, maintaining the address preset slightly concave wrist position all the way through the exercise.
- When you are sure you can advance in this most important exercise then do so adding a little clubhead weight or a longer club. Make sure you're darn careful as you do not want tendonitis in your wrist or elbow area.

Purpose

- Promotes one of the most important foundations in the entire game.
- Improves much needed strength of your hands, wrists, and forearms.
- Promotes just by exercise better pressure point positions of your right wrist and left-bowed wrist at impact.
- Promotes the necessary de-lofting of the golf club and longer flat spot.
- Helps reduce stress and injury potential in all these important areas.

THE PREPRACTICE AND PREROUND WARM-UP

These warm-up exercises are used to not just warm the body up for safety preparing to practice or play but finally promote intelligent body movement that is discussed in this material. I not only over the years have found these helpful but have seen the positive and accelerated game enhancement influence in all players. So please do not write these off.

1. Warm the body by swinging two clubs slowly together with smart, well-controlled movements. Ten swings both right and left handed to promote both sides of the body. Do these correctly by feeling correct plane loads as everything done right will translate.

2. Next overhead reach and side stretch that stretches the chest, lats, shoulders, and rotator muscles. Add slight back leans to open up the lower back.

3. Shoulder rotators with one club making 360-degree circles with each arm and shoulder. Ten swings both directions and with both left and right hand.

4. Lat stretches reaching out and stretching with a golf club both to the left and to the right, releasing the lats and lower-back area

5. Hamstring and lower-back stretch. With feet together and legs/knees straight allow your upper body to hang as you slowly reach toward your toes. Keep your upper and lower back straight and your shoulder rotators in place. Start this slow every day even at home, and gradually allow your hamstrings to soften as you eventually are able to reach the ground. This simple stretch is in the category of the most important stretches you must do every single day, whether you play or not.

6.   Wrist impact promotion exercise and strengthening.

7. The all-important pelvic hip hold and continuous shoulder turn
    drill. With an iron having the grip end on your target side lying
    across your shoulders and in a normal postured address position,
    rotate into a well-held and supported backswing hip position that
    we have spoken of so much in this book. Feel that right hip and
    left hip hold their pelvic flexes as you turn your shoulders on the
    correct shoulder plane with the grip end pointed at the ball line.
    Return to the proper well held impact position with the pelvic
    hip hold still in place and the target side leg posted solid and tall.
    Continue a bit into the follow thru feeling the stretch and well held
    pelvis. If you have a balloon, ball, or a large rolled up towel to use
    for this drill as discussed earlier, it should not be slipping around
    but held well in place during this motion.

All these warm-up drills should be accomplished each time you warm-up for your practice and or warm-up for your play. If they are initiated in the beginning positively correct in their positions and training, then you will inch your way toward sound movements. Do them well and make it a habit to do them always. You will not be disappointed at the outcome.

8. Finish with ten smooth, right-handed golf swings and then ten left to prepare your body to play. These eight special golf training warm-up exercises are not inclusive but are given to you to promote some important golf swing building positions that I have found accelerate development.

ACKNOWLEDGMENTS

While this project took a good deal of time and effort by many folks, I wanted to take a few minutes to thank many of the people that have not only helped in putting my words to paper, but also thank many who have had influence in my life.

I want to thank my wife Susie who has walked right alongside me all these years assisting me in every area of life and this golf career. She is the epitome of Proverbs 31 and the best friend a person could ever have.

I want to thank my son Mark who has helped me not only in this project, but for many years in every area of the golf instructional field.

I am very grateful to Molly Aronson, who did a ton of the editing of this work right in the middle of University finals. Special thanks to Steve Wehrley for some of the photography work and all the incredible time you spent making this happen. Also all the staff at TerraLago Golf Club for affording me the opportunity to instruct each winter at such a wonderful place and for all the friendships. I would like to let the men that are called the "Band of Brothers," Jim Hiskey, Billy Rogers, Peter Hiskey, Todd Howard, Wally Armstrong, Tony Krebs, Jim Barker, KB, Patrick Q, Todd Whiteman, Josh Olson, Jason Embler, Joe Lu, Vincent Kan, Troy Cheng, Jenson, Hi Long, Nishi san, Michi, the Nakajima family, Terry Olson, Matt Park, Mike Paxton, Dan Paulson, Steve Budinich, Ron Foote, Michael Putnam, Matt Park, Pastor Chuck, and all my brothers in Japan, Hong Kong, China, Argentina, and Korea. Without them, I would not be even close to the man I am fast trying to become. Thank you to the many students I used as models at home and in the Desert. Without you, all this work wouldn't happen.

I want to thank Dr. Paul Callaway who had huge influence in my instruction/life and influenced me to diligently study the effects of the body's relationship to golf. I will never forget "structure has a great deal to do with performance."

Thank you to the hundreds of teachers and mental performance experts around the world. I have learned and gleaned so much from every one of you. What I appreciate most is your willingness to allow me into your lives, teach alongside you, drop your guard, pick your brains, and answer so many of my questions. Special thanks to the many tour players who most started as very young students and progressed into fine young men and women of significance. You still keep me alongside and I am eternally grateful. I'd like to thank Dr. Mark Clarkson, who has been with me for near the entire journey with golf wisdom and grace.

How can I thank properly all the amateur students, juniors, college players, and parents who have entrusted me with their golf games and their children's golf games? To each of you, I owe so much.

I dedicate this book also to all the men and women in Japan, Korea, Argentina, and China whom I have the honor to teach and also work in the instructional trenches with for all these wonderful years. The Mizuno family, Misato and Akito, Keigo Tsuchiya, Takashi Ohara, Yoshi Hatanaka, Noriko Takahashi, Tetsuji Enya, Kojima san, Nakamura san, Takahashi san, Jun san, and over one hundred awesome teachers in Japan that I love dearly. Domo Arigato Gozimas! You have made a huge impact in my growth as a man and instructor.

To my wonderful kids who are the delight of my life, Mark, Karen, Jenny, and LB. You have made my life a beautiful one indeed and a great joy to wake up each day. To Seve, Joey, Bri, Tobs, and Mike. You are a joy to my soul. I'd like to thank the many college coaches across America, who have all had such a wonderful influence.

Most important of all is my Lord and Savior Jesus Christ who made the decision to call and rescue a man like me and change me from inside out. May my life and every step I take bring a smile to your face as I represent and share Your love for mankind on this earth. Thank you for the honor and privilege.

Joe Thiel Proverbs 3:5+6